The Manor and Cottages

Albemarle Park, Asheville, North Carolina

A Historic Planned Residential Community

Written and edited by
Jane Gianvito Mathews, AIA, and Richard A. Mathews

including
The Landscape of Albemarle Park: Samuel Parsons' Vision

by
Charles A. Birnbaum, ASLA

Graphic Design by Bernie Wolf

Research Assistance by Douglas R. Campbell, AIA

published by
The Albemarle Park-Manor Grounds Association, Inc.
Asheville, North Carolina

Manufactured in the United States of America.

First Edition.

10 9 8 7 6 5 4 3 2

The research of historical materials and the publication of this book was supported in part by grants from the Design Initiatives Program of the North Carolina Arts Council, the Terence L. Mills Preservation Services Fund of the National Trust for Historic Preservation, the Dogwood Fund of the Community Foundation of Western North Carolina, and the Marion Stedman Covington Foundation.

ISBN 0-9630437-0-6

Mathews, Jane Gianvito, 1954–
        The manor and cottages : Albemarle Park, Asheville, North Carolina : a historic planned residential community / written and edited by Jane Gianvito Mathews and Richard A. Mathews ; including The landscape of Albemarle Park : Samuel Parson's vision by Charles A. Birnbaum.
        p.   cm.
        Includes bibliographical references and index.
        ISBN 0-9630437-0-6 : $14.95
        1. Albemarle Park-Manor Grounds Assoc. 2. Architecture, Domestic--North Carolina--Asheville. 3. Planned communities--North Carolina--Asheville. 4. Asheville (N.C.)--Buildings, structures, etc.
        I. Mathews, Richard A. (Richard Alan), 1953–   . II. Title.
        NA9051.M38   1991
        728'.09756'88--dc20   91-31114
                                                                     CIP

Front & Back Cover: Adapted from an early Manor promotional brochure, ca. 1910. Brochure courtesy of Fred Kahn; graphic design by Bernie Wolf; calligraphy by Karen Palmer.

A postcard view of The Manor Inn, ca. 1903.

The entrance to Albemarle Park, looking up Cherokee Road from the Lodge.

Table of Contents

lanned with thoughtful attention to comfort, as understood in that day, with originality, and care in every detail, there was also about it an excellence and solidity of construction—and there was even something more. In the ample eaves, and slight touches of beauty permitted here and there, one might guess the builder's generous nature, and his desire to live easily and well. In the perfection of adjustment within the limited space at his command—in the gracious curve of a path, in the nice placing of a shrub, in the art of a concealing hedge, in the right form of a trellis, spoke the delicate heritage from his French ancestors which we call "taste." More than mere taste, it bespoke a perception of beauty, a clearness in design, an essential feeling for rightness and balance, that must be characteristic of the true artist.

(Mary Raoul Millis, <u>The Family of Raoul</u>)

William Greene Raoul. ca. 1899, at the time of his presidency of the Mexican National Railway.

The Early Years

"In 1886 we spent the summer in a large boarding house in Asheville, North Carolina. Mother had taken the children to walk from the boarding house to the farm on Charlotte Street. She stopped to get some milk from the farmer Deaver, and they sat by the spring house to drink it, and the children fed the fish in the near-by pond. Mother was captivated with the place, sensing its possibilities as a permanent summer home. The plan appealed to Father, and the purchase was made. Mr. Deaver's small farm house was converted into a temporary residence for the family.

"The plan was that we should go for one summer and live in the existing farm house, while the decision was being made as to the style and location of our own home."

The new place would sit "on the slopes of the hills above Charlotte Street, facing west, whence the gorgeous sunsets of Carolina could be admired in all their glory.

"We did not know that when we should return in the summer of 1887 this farm house in Asheville would be the only home we possessed." (Mary Raoul Millis, <u>The Family of Raoul</u>)

It was September, 1886.

William Greene Raoul was the President of the Central Railroad of Georgia and he had been sending his family away from Savannah each summer since 1880 to escape the city's oppressive climate. One year they went to Warm Springs, North Carolina. Another, to Martha's Vineyard.

He and his wife, Mary, now were raising seven children and, soon, there would be three more (an eleventh child, Edward, died at the age of two in December, 1882). Finding lodging for them all was becoming increasingly difficult.

"If our destination lay in one of the southern states, it had been his practice to put the entire family on the private car (C.R.R. No. 99), and transport us with the least complication, and with the least effort to provide the baby (there was always a baby) with fresh milk en route. The decision to adopt Asheville seemed to have solved the Summer Problem; there was to be no further trouble. But, alas, he had reckoned without engaging a boarding house!

"The plan was to leave the children, all seven or eight, in the car while Mother and Father were to go out and engage board. And so it was arranged. We had come up early

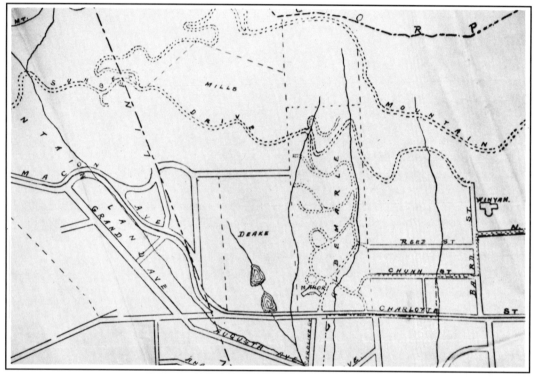

Portion of H. F. Grant's 1900 map of Asheville, showing the location of The Manor Inn and the road system of the Raouls' "Asheville Place," Albemarle Park.

place. Then, life could settle into a pleasant routine. They would bring their burgeoning family here each summer to enjoy the mountain air and the cosmopolitan social life, and return to Savannah in October when the climate in Georgia was once again bearable.

This placid and orderly life was not to be, however.

In less than four months, Raoul would lose a bitter stockholders' battle and be ousted from the Presidency of the Central. A rapid turn of events would force him to move his family to New York City and ten years would elapse before he returned to Asheville.

The next time he came he would have completely different plans for his Asheville Place.

"After the move to New York, all of our old summer plans...were thrown into the discard, and Asheville lay dormant for the family of Raoul, if not for its own people. Soon after our family left Asheville, we thought forever, things began to happen there.

"The Battery Park Hotel grew and flourished, and attracted notice as the one first class hotel of the lovely North Carolina mountain region. The improved railroad facilities brought people from far and near. Some medical man from the North decided that our mountain air had great therapeutic value for the ailing; and was the very best climate in the Eastern United States for the cure of tuberculosis.

"About this time a young man by the name of George Vanderbilt came to the Battery Park Hotel, and fell in love with the

from Spartanburg, and there were a number of acceptable boarding houses. The children were left in the car, and, on this particularly hot day, the Parents started out. One house after another was visited—plenty of rooms, yes. But, 'How many children have you, Mr. Raoul?' When the ungodly number was announced, the answer was always the same, they could not take them. At last, Father squared himself off opposite one of the landladies, and said, 'Well, Madam, just tell me how many you will take, and I will kill the balance!'

"However, we all survived this; and we all liked Asheville, with its dirt streets, board sidewalks, and Roman stepping stones across the mud." (Thomas Wadley Raoul, The Family of Raoul)

The Deaver farm on Charlotte Street just north of the city would provide the perfect solution, Raoul thought. The next summer, they would return to build their ideal summer beauty of this country. He started the purchase of land that was to become his Biltmore Estate.

"These happenings, with others of a minor nature, were enough to set off Real Estate Boom Number 1 for Asheville. An electric street car system was built, one of the first in America; a steam dummy line up Sunset Mountain; and the first Kenilworth Inn. A true boom, which fell with the inevitable thud of all booms! Its rise, its life, and its death consumed about eight years—say from 1888 to 1896.

"During that decade the little farm could have been sold for many times the ten thousand dollars which it cost. Father might have sold it, but Mother, who always loved the mountains, and was always an optimist about real estate values, never wanted to sell, and they never did sell. So, for ten years, the little farm lay idle and useless. Its value went down and there it lay, as we thought, useless for ever." (Thomas Wadley Raoul, <u>The Family of Raoul</u>)

When William Greene Raoul returned to Asheville in July, 1897, two things were uppermost in his mind—his son Thomas' poor health and his neglected piece of property on Charlotte Street.

Thomas had been stricken with tuberculosis a year earlier and his condition hadn't noticeably improved after a season in the dry desert climate out west. Perhaps the curative nature of Asheville's mountain air would be more effective for him.

And, since he was back in Asheville, it

The Battery Park Hotel, built in 1886 on top of Battery Porter Hill, was Asheville's premier hotel prior to The Manor's construction.

was time to do something with the farm he and Mary had bought.

Asheville's economy was in miserable shape in 1897. The city had gone through a relentless boom, beginning with the arrival of the railroad in 1880, and now, the bubble had finally burst.

Two local banks had failed, others were dealing in scrip, and the real estate market had gone bust.

The only way he would be able to make any money from his investment, he figured, would be by cutting up the farm into reasonably sized building lots and selling them off individually. Perhaps building some houses on some of them would make them more attractive.

From this simple thought, Albemarle Park emerged.

Entrance to Battery Park Hotel.
ASHEVILLE, N. C.

"One day Father and I were sitting on the porch of the Battery Park Hotel, with Colonel Frank Coxe, its owner, talking over our plan. Colonel Coxe said that the one thing that could be sold or rented in Asheville was a boarding house." (Thomas Wadley Raoul, The Family of Raoul)

Asheville in "The Gilded Age"

"Father always said that the mountain region of North Carolina was the only logical summer resort for that great hot country reaching from the Gulf of Mexico along the coast through Virginia, and he always had faith in its ultimate development.

"During our life in Savannah the ever present problem was where to take the ever increasing family for the summer.

"In those days, it was considered most unwise, from the standpoint of health, as well as comfort, to keep little children during the summers in the damp, hot, climate of Savannah. Accordingly, all who were able to afford it, made pilgrimages to higher altitudes for four, five, or even six months. The first year of our residence in Savannah, my Mother attempted to remain at home until July first; but this proved so unsatisfactory—crying, fretful, ailing babies, an exhausted mother, ragged tempers—that June first was fixed thenceforward as date for the Hegira. School began October first. We always spent September at Great Hill. Thus, there were three months during which the large family had to be maintained at an hotel,

Calling itself "The Journal of Society," The Asheville News and Hotel Reporter chronicled the activities of the many illustrious visitors to Asheville's grand hotels and boarding houses.

with all the attendant expense of clothes, transportation, and so on." (Mary Raoul Millis & Thomas Wadley Raoul, **The Family of Raoul**)

The Raouls first discovered the mountains of North Carolina in 1881, when they spent the Summer at Warm Springs (today called Hot Springs).

When they returned in 1886, this time to spend the entire summer in Asheville, the city was a thriving vacation and health resort center.

"The Gilded Age" was reaching its height at this time and wealthy travellers from all over the east were coming to the resort

hotels, health spas and elaborate inns that dotted the mountains, to delight in the healthful climate and the cosmopolitan atmosphere.

Asheville's local businessmen and civic leaders promoted the city as a haven for both the urbane and the infirm, advertising its healthful atmosphere and its pure water to people far and wide.

In 1899, real estate dealer J.M. Campbell published Asheville, Nature's Sanitarium, to attract people to Asheville and to promote his real estate services.

"Asheville is the metropolis of Western North Carolina; the impregnable fortress against pulmonary troubles; the consumptive's safest refuge and the invalid's best physician.

The original Kenilworth Inn, ca. 1890, where Thomas Wadley Raoul often joined friends for a good dinner and lively conversation. It was destroyed by fire in 1909.

"Eminent doctors state emphatically that they know of no spot in Europe so desirable as a health resort as the country around Asheville. The climate is a specific for incipient phthisis. Asheville is now the established and most noted health and pleasure resort in America. It is the mecca of the Southron as he flees from the mosquito, heat and malaria of the Southern Summer, and the dream of the Northerner as he shivers from the blizzards of the North and West. Here tubercular con-sumption is not hereditary, and malaria is unknown."

In 1882, the Board of Trade was created, precursor to today's Chamber of Commerce, and it produced a steady stream of promotional brochures which were sent forth across the country, advertising Asheville as the perfect place to visit and to live. It stressed the sophisticated social climate that existed here.

From a Board of Trade booklet published in 1898:

"It is a matter of common remark from those who visit Asheville that they always meet people whom they know. A few years ago a census of one of the public school buildings, containing 500 pupils, was taken, to see how many of the pupils were born in Asheville. Of the total number, just 86 could speak of Asheville as their birthplace. This will give an idea of how cosmopolitan this city of 18,000 people is. There is probably not a state in the Union, not a civilized country on the globe, that has not furnished its quota of wide-awake citizens to Asheville's brisk intellectual and commercial atmosphere. Where nature has been so lavish in her gifts of indescribable and varied scenery and in her clear, bracing climate, it would be strange if the people here were unmindful of their advantages and were not making a city in keeping with the perfect surroundings.

"And so, elegantly equipped hotels are here, ranking with the best in the country, catering to seekers of health, pleasure and recreation, and patronized by thousands of visitors. Among these are the Battery Park, Kenilworth Inn, The Manor, Hotel Berkeley, Swannanoa, Oaks, Glen Rock, Asheville, Arcadia and Western."

"Scores of home-like boarding houses are here; excellent flats, and beautiful private residences, occupied by refined and cultured people, many of whom are persons of wealth.

"What Asheville is:

"It is not out of touch with the day's doings, for New York papers are read here at breakfast next morning.

"It is not full of half dead people, but is alive with energy and ozone, a stimulus to mind, body and estate.

"It is the center of a circle embracing the territory bounded by the Mississippi River, the Gulf of Mexico, the Atlantic Ocean, and the Great Lakes. No other resort draws from so wide a field."

There had been hotel service in Asheville as early as 1814, when the Eagle Hotel was built just down from the Public Square on south Main Street (Biltmore Avenue today).

While other hotels opened through the years to serve the growing numbers of merchants and other travellers coming through town on the Buncombe Turnpike—the Buck Hotel on North Main Street, the Bank Hotel, and others—it was the building of the Grand Central Hotel in 1878 at the corner of Patton and Lexington Avenues that signalled the beginning of the hotel building boom that continued into the 1920s.

The grandest hotel of the era was the Battery Park Hotel which opened on July 12, 1886 and sprawled atop 25 acres of landscaped grounds on Battery Porter Hill in the center of the city.

It had modern bathrooms with hot and cold water, elevators, ballrooms, dining rooms, a bowling alley and separate billiards rooms for the men and the ladies.

Colonel Frank Coxe, the Battery Park's owner, recognized that Asheville's moderate climate would allow an innkeeper to operate all year 'round, attracting people both from the sultry Southern cities in the summer and

The Knickerbocker, ca.1899, was one of Asheville's popular boarding houses serving summer tourists. It was located at the corner of E. College and Davidson Streets, where the Buncombe County Courthouse sits today.

from the frigid Northern cities each winter. His success spurred yet further growth.

The Swannanoa Hotel (1880), the Oakland Heights Hotel and Baths (1887), later known as the Victoria Inn, and the Kenilworth Inn (1890) were several of the other majestic hotels in Asheville at that time that also did a brisk business.

Competing with them for guests were several dozen boarding houses spread across the city, including the Knickerbocker, the

Rock Ledge and Thomas Wolfe's mother's place, the Old Kentucky Home.

The Raouls had stayed at the Battery Park soon after it opened in 1886.

Eleven years later, when William Greene Raoul and his son, Thomas, finally decided to build their own grand hotel, The Manor Inn, on the land they owned on Charlotte Street, they had a good knowledge of their competition.

The Great Hill Place, at Bolingbroke, Georgia, was William Morrill Wadley's country estate which became the center of activities each September for the Raouls from the early 1870s into the 1920s. It was destroyed by fire on January 31, 1982.

Mary Wadley Raoul, ca. 1900, mother of eleven children, joined her husband as a leader of various progressive community endeavors. The hundreds of family letters written to her provide an illustrative portrait of the significant activities of the Raoul family members.

The Family of Raoul

"Let me affirm that our Parents were both exceptional people; each outstanding, each strong in his own right, each a vivid, dramatic figure, impressing his personality upon his environment." (Mary Raoul Millis, <u>The Family of Raoul</u>)

William Greene Raoul and his wife, Mary, set a high standard for themselves and their children as they rose to prosperity in the post Civil War South. The impact of their progressive activities as important civic leaders in Macon, Atlanta, Asheville and across the nation can still be measured today.

By 1890, William Greene Raoul had become an internationally respected railroad man, known for his high ethical standards and for having helped rebuild the Central of Georgia after the devastation of the Civil War. He also is credited with rescuing the Southwestern Railroad from bankruptcy in the late 1870s.

His greatest success came when he was elected President of the Mexican National Railroad, hired to save it from an impending international scandal and build it into a thriving railroad in the West.

William Greene Raoul was born in Independence, Louisiana, outside of New Orleans

William Green Raoul, at The Manor, ca. 1899.

in 1843, the son of a prosperous trader who operated schooners on Lake Ponchartrain and in the Mississippi River delta region.

His grandfather, Francois Guillaume Raoul De Champmanoir, left France around 1793 to escape the convulsions that were consuming the country at the time and settled in the West Indies where he became a land owner and operated a plantation. To escape an insurrection of the slaves on the island of San Domingo, he moved to New Orleans, where he married and operated a hotel in the French Quarter. When he died in 1825, William's

The Raoul family residence, at 708 Peachtree Street in Atlanta, Georgia, designed by Bradford L. Gilbert in 1890. Still standing, along with two outbuildings, it is in great disrepair and is an endangered landmark.

father, twelve at the time, was sent to live with relatives in Springfield, Louisiana.

It was in this area northwest of New Orleans that William Greene Raoul was to meet his future wife and father-in-law and begin the steady progress toward the Presidency of the Mexican National Railroad.

In 1857, when he was only fourteen years old, Raoul met and became awestruck by William Morrill Wadley, a prominent railroad man from Georgia who had brought his family to nearby Amite, Louisiana. The Raouls and the Wadleys quickly became close friends, and developed a life-long partnership that would bond them together during the travails of the next ten years and would help them face the struggles imposed by the Civil War and its aftermath.

When the war came, young William joined the Washington Artillery of New Orleans to serve the Confederacy. He was in the Pennsylvania campaign, saw action at Gettysburg and was a witness to Pickett's Charge. He was 19 years old.

After the war, the enormous task of resurrecting the South from the devastation it caused began. It was decided that the Car Works that William's father had operated in Independence during the war would be rebuilt and operated jointly as Raoul Sons & Wadley. Though it eventually failed in 1870, it prepared William Greene Raoul for his long career as a railroad man.

In 1868, the Wadley family was united with the Raouls when William Greene Raoul married Mary Millen Wadley.

After the Car Works failed, Raoul slowly began working himself up through the ranks of the Central of Georgia to which his father-in-law had returned. He began by building woodsheds and other support structures along the line to serve the trains travelling by. Soon, he was promoted to Assistant Roadmaster. In January, 1875, he became the Roadmaster, and, in 1883, after Wadley's death, he was elected president of the Central.

By this time, the Raouls were raising six children, and they had become active community leaders.

While they lived in Macon in the late 1870s, they established the first Kindergarten in Georgia. Mary Raoul had heard of the "children's gardens" that existed up North, and, with her husband's support, she decided to create one for the people of Macon.

That she had five children underfoot at the time and that they couldn't begin elementary school until age six or seven likely was more than sufficient reason to encourage her to take on this endeavor. Later, when she moved to Atlanta, she continued her activities in this area and played an active role in the Free Kindergarten movement. One of the city's early kindergartens was named after her.

William, meanwhile, was in a bitter ethical battle as president of the Central.

"While he [Wadley] lived, the ownership of the road was still vested in the people of Georgia; that is, the stock was held in comparatively small blocks, by people scattered all over the state. The annual meeting...was an event of state-wide interest. The stock-

The sons of Mary Wadley and William Greene Raoul, ca. 1904. From left, William Greene, Jr., Thomas, Gaston, Norman, and Loring.

Mary Millen Raoul, ca. 1900, authored <u>The Family of Raoul</u> in 1945, a memoir that documents the activities and contributions of the entire Raoul family.

ests than primarily for the benefit of the small stockholders and the growth of the state.

"The issue was fairly understood to be whether the Central of Georgia, greatest enterprise of the state, should be owned by numbers of the plain people within the state or by "foreign" interests, seated afar among the Bankers of New York. During the succeeding four years, the struggle raged, more or less openly, until, in 1887, the tide had turned, and our party was defeated." (Mary Raoul Millis, <u>The Family of Raoul</u>)

William Greene Raoul lost his battle and was ousted from the presidency.

In less than six months, however, he was offered the presidency of the Mexican National Railroad, a position that would bring him international fame and establish him as one of the most prominent railroad men of his time.

Construction of the Mexican National had begun in 1881 and it was supposed to run from Laredo, Texas to the City of Mexico. At the time Raoul took the reins, the project had collapsed, 500 miles of the railroad remained to be built, and the entire project was threatened by foreclosure.

Raoul led the effort to save the company and succeeded in getting the line completed in just twelve months.

This success permanently established his reputation, providing him quite a measure of wealth and elevating his family to the pinnacle of society.

In early 1888, as fortunes shifted, the family moved away from Savannah,

Georgia—where Mary always felt slightly spurned by the established aristocracy—to New York City, home of the headquarters of the Mexican National.

After first staying in hotels in Manhattan, they moved to Staten Island, and rented "the Mayo Place," known as Moss Bank, a large estate near Fort Wadsworth. A year later, they moved to Krebs House in Brighton, overlooking the ferry landing.

By 1890, Raoul had had enough of New York and northern sensibilities, and decided it was time to return to Georgia and build a home for his family in Atlanta. He and Mary now had ten children ranging from their new infant son, Norman, to twenty year old William Greene, Jr.

As president of the Mexican National, William Greene Raoul spent very little time with his family. Most of it was spent travelling between his office in New York City and the family home on Peachtree Street in Atlanta; along the Mexican National Railroad in the Southwest overseeing operations; or visiting his many children as they established themselves in business or marriage in different parts of the country.

It fell to his wife, Mary, to provide the necessary stability for the large family and keep matters organized. By the time they established themselves in the Peachtree house, the Raouls were one of the premier families in Atlanta. The children were growing up and preparing for their own lives.

As her five daughters grew older, Mary Raoul coordinated their debuts in Atlanta

holders had the privilege of a free ride on their own road to the scene of the meeting—Savannah—and they voted, like freemen and owners, for the officers who should manage their property.

"A certain group of Georgians, very influential men, designed to concentrate the ownership of the railroad stock in the hands of a few people, in order to direct the policies of the road rather towards their own financial intersociety, and then the marriages that followed.

She monitored the health of Thomas and Rosine, her two children who were struck down by tuberculosis, as they travelled to different parts of the world seeking a cure.

She regularly corresponded with all of her adult children after they had moved away—to Seattle, Chattanooga, Asheville, the Phillipines—and kept her husband informed about their activities.

As the size of the family remaining at home dwindled, Mary Raoul became increasingly active in Atlanta society. She served on the Board of the Cotton States & International Exposition in 1895, was a member of the Daughters of the American Revolution and the United Daughters of the Confederacy, and, with her daughter, Eleonore, was very active in the Woman's Suffrage movement.

"Mother's pleasure in social affairs was now to a certain extent transferred to the larger interests of the community. Always an ardent proponent of the rights of women, she became an enthusiastic advocate of the Woman's Suffrage movement. She gave both money and time to the campaign in Georgia and Atlanta, finding great happiness in the companionship of Eleonore in this most vital work.

"After suffrage had been won, the organization in Atlanta was one of the first to set up a League of Women Voters. During the years of struggle, Eleonore had been one of the leaders in the cause. In this, as has been observed, she was ably assisted by Mother, who gave most generous financial aid for many years. Indeed, it is safe to say that it is

Thomas Wadley Raoul and his friend, Mr. Gillidance, with a bobcat they had just killed near Oracle, Arizona, during one of Thomas' trips out west in search of relief from his tuberculosis.

largely due to the labor and money of these two forward-looking women, that the Atlanta League today holds the place of influence which it occupies, both nationally and locally." (Mary Raoul Millis, The Family of Raoul)

During much of the Raouls' life, William Wadley's Great Hill Place, in Bolingbroke, Georgia, had been the focus for the family's activities. In the early years, when times were tough, the Raouls resided there until they could establish themselves in Macon. Later,

they vacationed there for at least a month each year. Through the years, William Greene Raoul had built a rustic springhouse and other small structures on the grounds.

With the development of Albemarle Park, William Greene Raoul and the family finally had the opportunity to build their own Raoul family retreat. This time, though, instead of small springhouses and other secondary structures, they had the chance to put their skills and talents to use building a first class resort hotel and a collection of exquisite "cottages."

Bradford L. Gilbert, ca. 1900, architect of Albemarle Park.

The Architect & "The Asheville Place"

"Organizer, Administrator, Craftsman, Artist—Father was all of these. Beauty delighted his soul—especially beauty of line and form; the beauty of fine craftsmanship, and the harmony of good design. In Mr. Gilbert, he found an understanding friend. Together they worked with great happiness; and together they built a lovely and a perfect house." (Mary Raoul Millis, <u>The Family of Raoul</u>)

The farm that the Raouls bought in 1886 just north of the city was roughly 42 acres in size. They purchased it from Reuben M. Deaver, a major landowner and speculator in Buncombe County, who had bought it himself just three years earlier.

It was being used as a tenant farm at the time, the lower portion at the west end given over to grazing land for cattle and the upper end left wooded.

There was a small, one-acre pond at the western end that was most likely created when Charlotte Street was built and the streams coming down off Sunset Mountain were dammed in order to provide a level road surface.

Judging from the maps of that time, Sunset Drive was the only road that crossed the property, up in the steeper wooded hillside area. Reed and Chunn Streets probably ended in cul-de-sacs at the southern edge of the property, or dwindled into dirt trails that ended at the bank of the creek that came down off Sunset Mountain and fed the pond.

The original plan was to build a summer home on the site that was large enough for the entire family. Though this plan was never carried out and the farm remained unchanged, Raoul never entirely forgot about his "Asheville place."

In the beginning, he was content to just rent the farm out, letting a local real estate agent manage it for him.

In 1890, though, while he was working with New York architect Bradford Gilbert on the details of the family house he was building in Atlanta, he also began to explore various options for his farm in Asheville.

After all, these were the boom days in Asheville and land speculation was rampant. Anyone with money was buying land looking to turn it around quickly for an easy profit. The Raouls hadn't been back to Asheville for three years now, and it looked like they never would return, so he began to think about ways to recapture his original investment and make a tidy profit while the boom lasted.

The Manor and cottages, ca. 1910, as viewed from an undeveloped hill to the west of Albemarle Park between today's Edwin Place and Hillside Street.

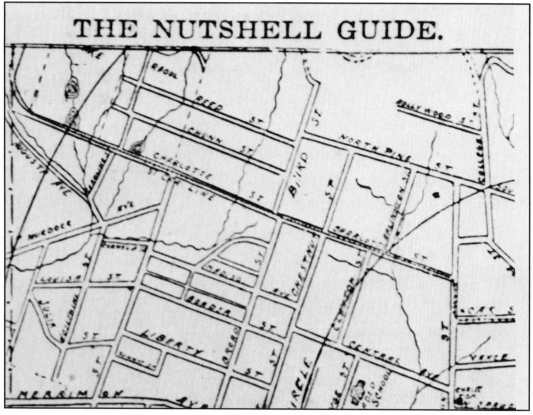

An early map of Asheville showing the Raoul land before any work was done. The pond is visible at Charlotte Street. The roads that are indicated here as crossing the property only existed on paper at this time.

By August, 1890, he was thinking about subdividing the 42 acres into smaller parcels that would be more attractive to buyers. He sent a map that had been drawn by the city surveyor, H. M. Ramseur, to Benjamin M. Lee, the City engineer, and, in his correspondence, discussed different possible approaches he could take in cutting the property up into smaller building lots.

After looking at the map, Raoul saw that the Charlotte Street frontage was greater than he originally thought, and he judged he might be able to create four lots there. His main concern was where Chunn and and Reed Streets lay as they approached his property from the south, and whether there was enough room to have back-to-back building lots between Charlotte and Chunn Streets. His interest was to maximize the potential of his property and make the lots more attractive for sale.

By 1893, he had consulted with several real estate people in Asheville. One of these advisors, H. F. Grant, recommended cutting the property into two large parcels, creating a lower property adjacent to Charlotte Street, and a separate, mountainside property to the east, with access from Sunset Drive.

Nothing came of these plans, though, and the farm remained relatively unchanged from when they bought it.

The Architect of Albemarle Park—Bradford Gilbert

Bradford Lee Gilbert was the logical choice for the architect of Albemarle Park. He and Raoul had worked well together on previous railroad projects and, judging from the letters Raoul was often writing him offering suggestions and making recommendations, Gilbert was willing to let the client be an active participant in the design process.

Gilbert was born into a prominent family in Watertown, New York, in 1853. Instead of going to Yale College, which was the family tradition and had been expected of him, he decided he would become an architect.

It was the tradition at that time to learn

The Virginia Beach Hotel, ca. 1887, later called The Princess Anne Hotel, in Virginia Beach, Virginia, was one of the many public buildings designed by Gilbert in association with railroad companies.

The Tower Building, ca. 1889, the first "skyscraper" in New York City.

the craft of architecture and building on the job, under a master's instruction, rather than in the classrooms of a university.

So, in 1872, he became a student in the office of J. Cleveland Cady, a prominent New York City architect of the period, and learned his trade while working on Cady's projects.

After five years under Cady's tutelage, he was appointed the official architect to the New York, Lake Erie and Western Railroad.

The experience he gained in designing railroad stations and other buildings along the lines of this railroad system gave him enough confidence to open his own office, specializing in the design of railroad stations and other kindred structures. He was only 29 at the time.

His career blossomed quickly, and he began building structures for numerous railroads across the country. Working for the wealthy railroad barons of the time, it was only natural that he would also be called upon to design their private clubs, their hotels and their mansions.

His most prominent buildings include the Berkeley Arms Hotel in Berkeley, New Jersey (1883), the Peninsular Club House in Grand Rapids, Michigan (1883-4), the Riding Club in New York City (1885-6), and the Virginia Beach Hotel in Virginia Beach, Virginia (1888).

Much of his civic and railroad work is reminiscent of H.H. Richardson's, with romanesque arches over doorways and windows and rusticated stonework, and is described in the architectural journals of the

William Greene Raoul, Jr., the Raouls' eldest son, who worked in Bradford Gilbert's New York City architectural office in 1892.

time as having Flemish or English Renaissance influences.

Gilbert is most widely known for designing and receiving official approval to build the first real "skyscraper" in New York City.

In 1888, Gilbert was faced with the challenge of designing a fifteen story office building for a narrow lot at 50 Broadway that had

A well house at Great Hill Place designed by William Greene Raoul.

only twenty one feet, six inches of frontage.

Called "The Tower Building," it was the first building to receive a permit for the construction method in which a structural steel "skeleton" is utilized to support masonry "curtain walls".

It was completed in 1889, and, from its opening until 1908, Gilbert maintained his office on the top floor.

In Gilbert, William Greene Raoul found the perfect architect, someone with whom he could work closely, who could take his draw-ings and ideas and refine them into fully inte-grated designs.

Raoul probably felt a special kinship with Gilbert. They both began their careers in sim-ilar fashion, Gilbert developing his design skills on the secondary, outlying structures for the N.Y.L.E. & W. R.R., and Raoul expanding his own self-taught design abilities by build-ing similar small wood sheds and staging buildings for the Central of Georgia, as well as for the family estate at Great Hill.

"In collaboration with his friend, Bradford L. Gilbert, he became absorbed, delightedly, in drawing plans for his elabo-rate, beautiful, permanent home. Evening after evening, the huge sheets of drawing paper would be spread out on the dining table, and Father would spend hours meditat-ing on the dimensions of the rooms, positions of doors and windows; or else, with tiny bits of paper cut to scale [in the] shapes of beds, dressing tables, sofas, etc., would place and replace them in the rooms which they were to occupy, so that the best advantage might be obtained of lighting, roominess, convenience, and so on." (Mary Raoul Millis, The Family of Raoul)

Gilbert and Raoul had developed both a good working relationship and a close per-sonal friendship through the years. In 1892, Gilbert even employed the Raouls' eldest son, William Greene, Jr., in his New York City office. Judging from young William's letters at the time, it's obvious Gilbert didn't hire the young man for his exceptional skills, but,

rather, as a favor to his client, concerned about the welfare of his first born child.

Working with the Raouls allowed Gilbert to be more playful in his designing and gave him the freedom to experiment with different styles—Dutch Revival, Half-Timber Tudor, and the Shingle Style, which was at the height of its popularity at the time.

While it can't be reliably determined exactly which structures in Albemarle Park benefited from Bradford Gilbert's expertise after he designed the Lodge, Manor and first five cottages, a noticeable change in style can be detected in those cottages that were built after his death in 1911.

Thomas Wadley Raoul, ca. 1897, when he first began work on the development and construction of Albemarle Park.

The Lodge and the Manor Inn

"I came to Asheville primarily to regain my health, but as it was then thought important to keep up my interest in life, as part of the cure, Father hit on the plan of having me cut out and clear the Asheville Place with a view to the possibility of cutting it into building lots and selling it. At that time Charlotte Street was the ragged end of nowhere and, the boom having petered out shortly before, there was but little chance of selling the property. In August I began the clearing without then having decided how the development should be made." (Thomas Wadley Raoul, <u>The Family of Raoul</u>)

If William Greene Raoul was the "architect" of the concept of Albemarle Park, it was his third son, Thomas Wadley Raoul, who was to be the foreman of the project and the one who made the vision a reality and a success. For a period of almost twenty-five years, Thomas devoted his time and his energies to overseeing the construction and the management of The Manor and cottages.

"...In the fall of 1896, I was working for S.M. Inman & Co., cotton merchants, in Macon, Georgia. I was twenty years old. I had very little to do with sick people, and, as far

as I know, had never known a person with tuberculosis, or, as we generally called it, consumption. But, in that fall, while at Great Hill, that fatal disease struck. It mowed me down. As I thought then, it ended my life.

"At this point Father took over. He soon sent me off to the Great West, to breathe its health giving air that was to cure, if at all, without treatment.

"Leaving Atlanta in the fall of 1896, I went by way of Texas, California, Colorado, Mexico...and found myself back in Atlanta about July 1897. Atlanta was recognized as only a temporary stop on my way to health... and I was soon off for Asheville.

"One day Father and I were sitting on the porch at the Battery Park Hotel, with Colonel Frank Coxe, its owner, talking over our plan. We spoke of our plan to build a few cottages for sale, so as to make the surrounding land more valuable. Colonel Coxe said that the one thing that could be sold or rented in Asheville was a boarding house. Father and I both considered this out of the question for us, and we let it drop. Later, I moved my living quarters to Mrs. Glaser's boarding house, [at 244 East Chestnut Street] which was very attractive, and I began to change my mind about boarding houses. By the time I saw Father again,

The Manor Inn, soon after it opened on New Year's Eve, 1898. Thomas lived upstairs in the Lodge, in the foreground at Charlotte Street, and managed the operations of The Inn from his office downstairs in the turret. Clover and Milfoil cottages can be seen in the distance.

Thomas Wadley Raoul in Oracle, Arizona, with his dog, Stonewall, during one of his journeys in the West.

which was in Atlanta at Christmas, I told him that I had decided that the quickest way we could bring value to the property was to build a boarding house on it, as suggested by Colonel Coxe; that would attract more people more quickly than any other method. Father was receptive to the idea this time, and asked;

'But, if we build a boarding house and can't rent it, who will run it?' With the confidence of youth, I said I would.

"Father had consulted with his old friend, Bradford L. Gilbert, the New York architect, and, through him, with Mr. Samuel Parsons, Landscape Architect of Central Park, New York. They had made the tentative lay-out of the Asheville Place, which, up to this time, had no other name." (Thomas Wadley Raoul, The Family of Raoul)

According to Thomas, it was his Mother who, in early 1898, thought of the name, Albemarle Park. "The naming of real estate developments was by no means so general then as now, but our salesmanship foresaw that a name, and a good, dignified name at that, was essential to our project. Therefore, we went to the top, and borrowed from the Duke of Albemarle, one of those who held the original grant from the Crown to the land which was to become North Carolina." (Thomas Wadley Raoul, The Family of Raoul)

Thomas Wadley Raoul was only twenty years old when he began working on the construction of Albemarle Park and he was filled with enthusiasm for the project. He began by clearing and grubbing the land, surveying it and setting posts along the perimeter while he waited for instructions from Bradford Gilbert.

During his first few months in Asheville he was busy familiarizing himself with city government, negotiating on his Father's behalf for the sewer and water lines to be extended down Charlotte Street to Albemarle

Park. He was also involved in the incorporation of the Albemarle Park Company, the hiring of laborers and all the day-to-day work that was being done on site.

"The last few days of the past week I have spent in cording the wood, and much to my surprise find that I will have between 35 and 40 cords. I am afraid you will think I have skinned the place but I have not and I have not heard a single person say it is too thin. In fact I know it is much too thick to use but you can't tell where we will want a thick growth and where a lawn." (Thomas Wadley Raoul to his mother from the Battery Park Hotel, Sept. 4, 1897)

While Thomas was clearing the land, Bradford Gilbert had consulted with Samuel Parsons, Jr., Landscape Architect for the City of New York at the time, and brought him on board to develop a comprehensive site and landscape plan.

Gilbert was excited by the setting of the Raoul's land and challenged by its topography. With Parsons, he worked to develop the land's potential while maintaining its beauty. By the end of August, 1897, Gilbert had a three-dimensional wax plan made of the entire property so that Thomas could begin to lay out the network of roads that gently traversed the steep hillsides.

"By this time you have seen Mr. Gilbert and he has told you of the few hours spent here. He was very enthusiastic about the place and said it had the greatest possibilities for a place of its size. I tell you it made me want to get to the building to hear him talk of the houses he would put here and there. Mr. Gilbert thinks it would be a good plan to leave the pond where it is and have it cleaned out and a border of stone put about it. This I tried to persuade him out of, saying that I had no use for a pond in the South but he stuck to his idea." (Thomas Wadley Raoul to his mother from the Battery Park Hotel, Sept. 4, 1897)

Thomas' studies in engineering at the Georgia Institute of Technology stood him in good stead as he began laying out the roads in Albemarle Park, laying the drainage pipes and building retaining walls, and ultimately filling in the pond at Charlotte Street.

"In November 1897, Gaston and I, armed with transit, level, rod and chain, arrived at the Glaser boarding house to make a survey and road layout of Albemarle Park—Gaston as engineer, and I as rodman. 'Rodding' over mountain land would not now be considered exactly the cure for tuberculosis, but it was good enough for 1897, and perhaps as good as my Mexican cure. In any event I was determined that no one should know I was here for my health—a delusion and a mistake. But I kept it up pretty well till 1903.

"Before we had the roads even on paper, Father and Mr. Gilbert were busy with building plans. I remember Father telling me how the idea originated of having The Manor (it was Mr. Gilbert who gave it the name) built in two wings opening from the center toward the street. He and Mr. Gilbert were sitting at a dinner table opposite each other, and Father was illustrating with his hands, as he so often did, showing in which direction was the

The Lodge was the first structure built in Albemarle Park, erected in 1898 by James A. Tennent, the contractor who built the Asheville City Hall on the Public Square downtown. Charlotte Street was still unpaved at this time, but the electric street railway tracks had already been laid and there were streetcars that regularly passed by.

mountain view, when Mr. Gilbert said, 'I have it! We will build the house just as you sit.'— and so they did." (Thomas Wadley Raoul, The Family of Raoul)

Thomas and his father walked the land together and sited the first four buildings in late 1897. Construction began on the first of these, the Lodge (Gatehouse), in early 1898.

Designed by Gilbert in the Tudoresque shingle style with pebble-dash stucco at the first floor and a granite foundation, the Lodge arched over the entrance drive leading from Charlotte Street into Albemarle Park. During the early years of the development, the offices of the Albemarle Park Company were on the ground floor of the two-story shingle and

The original Manor Inn, ca. 1900, facing the western mountains from its hillside perch above Charlotte Street, before the addition of the 1903 wing.

stone turret, and Thomas lived in the rooms on the second floor.

The contractor's bid for this first structure came in at $2,000, considerably more than the Raouls had intended to spend. This sent Mr. Gilbert back to the drawing board in an attempt to reduce the cost.

This structure, and all the others built by the Raouls, were constructed of quality materials with the finest craftsmanship of the day, two things they valued highly.

They contracted with James A. Tennent, to construct the Lodge, indicating that if he worked satisfactorily they might contract with him for the other structures. Tennent was a prominent architect and builder in Asheville

at the time. He came to the city in 1871 from South Carolina and built some of the early municipal buildings in Asheville—the three-story County Courthouse (1876) and Asheville's City Hall on Court Square (1892). He also built several impressive residential structures—The Holland, a boarding house at 40 N. French Broad Avenue and the Jeter Pritchard House on Chestnut Street.

"More satisfactory results are always obtained by incorporating the general scheme for 'finishing and furnishing' in the design at the outset." (Bradford L. Gilbert, Architectural Sketches)

Throughout the construction of the Lodge, Thomas consulted with Bradford Gilbert on the details of construction, all the way down to the finishing of the plaster walls with paint, papers, and fabric. They established a good working relationship that continued as the construction of The Manor and the first two cottages, Columbus and Clover, was undertaken.

For The Manor, Thomas and his Father wanted to design an inn that architecturally and functionally would have original and unique features distinguishing it from the usual resort hotels of the day, against which they were competing for business. To this end, they chose a design that would evoke the atmosphere and all the comfort of an English country house.

"The Manor, open the year round, has many original and distinctive features which make it widely different from the usual hotels found in most resorts. It provides a perfectly comfortable place to live for a long or short time, attractive in its surroundings, complete but modest in its appointments, with the air of refinement essential to the comfort of cultivated people. Every effort is made to have the place as nearly like a home as a public house can well be, and in carrying out this idea, all the conventional hotel features which are not essential to a proper service are eliminated." (from an early promotional booklet for The Manor)

For instance there was no sign of office, newsstand, or clerk in the spacious foyer of The Manor. The accommodations for guests were usually arranged with Thomas in advance, and, after they had been settled in their rooms, they walked leisurely down to the Lodge, where all business was transacted. This left The Manor's public spaces entirely for the use of the guests.

The main entrance hall was dominated by a huge brick fireplace which was open on two sides and was equipped with immense andirons. It had a cobblestone hearth and triple inset niches above the mantle which held a collection of oriental vases. The room was furnished with lounge chairs and oak tables, and was more a casual living room than formal lobby.

The first dining room for the Inn was adjacent to the main lobby and sitting rooms and was furnished with tables and chairs that had a slight art nouveau flair, purchased from the Grand Rapids firm of Berkey & Gay, one of the leaders in the manufacture of furniture in the arts and crafts style.

In regards to the meals that The Manor provided, Thomas noted that "the difference from the usual hotel is especially marked in the table, which is very much like that of a well conducted private house. Elaborate French dishes are not provided and there are no printed menus, but the appetizing meals are thoroughly well cooked and daintily served by quiet and efficient waitresses. Distinctive Southern cooking is a feature of The Manor, and, together with the freshest of vegetables from the Company's farm, assures a very fine table."

Thomas prodded his Father to buy the small farm on Spooks Branch Road (north of the city, off Beaverdam Road) which supplied The Manor's produce. Though the farm was worked by hired staff, Thomas supervised the purchase of animals and the pruning and maintenance of the long neglected fruit trees he found on the site. Every few days he would find time in his busy schedule to ride his horse over to the farm to survey its progress, taking advantage of this suitable excuse to escape, for a while, the rigors of Manor business.

The original section of The Manor Inn, which provided twenty-five guest rooms on two floors and several staff rooms on the third, was constructed, like the Lodge, in the Tudoresque shingle style, characterized by the granite foundation and upper floors of heavy pegged timbered frames with rough pebble dash stucco infill and evenly coursed wood shingling. The design of the building is composed of an asymmetrical arrangement of various gable ends. As described in the National Register of Historic Places, "the northern gable represents a salt-box in appearance, the central gable is an overshot flared triangle supported on a two-story timbered bay, and the south gable is Dutch gambrel in form."

Seven chimneys of rough stone and brick accented these roof lines, three piercing the ridges and four projecting from the face of the building between the gable ends. One chimney featured a whimsical oval stained glass window decorated with flowers, vines, and a spider and web located in the original dining room, reputed to be designed by Tiffany.

The entire Raoul family helped develop Albemarle Park. Standing in front of Galax cottage, Norman, in white, and Loring survey the Fox Hall lot in preparation for its sale in 1913 to E. A. Fordtran, publisher of the New Orleans Times/Picayune newspaper.

The entrance to The Manor was on the north side where a porte cochere provided convenient, protected access for guests arriving by carriage.

The windows of the Inn have diamond-panes in the upper sashes and are often "eye-browed" with shingling. Exterior doors to the porches had beveled glass panes. The roofs of The Manor, unlike the cottages', which were layered with wood shingles, were covered with heavy red french diamond-cut composition shingles.

Together all these design elements "describe a wide, graceful arc giving the

The entrance to The Manor Inn was sheltered by this porte cochere. The windows of Peacock Alley are to the right.

slopes of Sunset Mountain."(from an early Manor brochure)

The public rooms of The Manor had richly carved and ornamented mouldings and cornices in wood and plaster. It is believed some of this work was executed by Italian workmen who had been brought to Asheville to work on the Biltmore Estate and decided to remain once that was completed.

When he began to work on the landscaping of the grounds, Thomas consulted with Chauncey D. Beadle at the Biltmore Estate nursery about the procurement of the plants on his lengthy planting lists and who should be hired to set them.

Though Thomas purchased many of the early plants for Albemarle Park from the Biltmore Estate, Beadle recommended that he have Mr. Deake do a lot of the planting for him, since he and his wife operated the Idlewild Green Houses and Floral Gardens just north of Albemarle Park, where Sunset Parkway is today.

On New Years' Eve, 1898, Thomas' labors were complete when The Manor Inn officially opened to immediate acclaim. This proved to be just the beginning of his education in resort hotel management and was only the first of many construction projects he would supervise in Albemarle Park during the next two decades.

Thomas had decided to be the "landlady," as he called it, and assume responsibility for the daily workings of The Manor and Albemarle Park. He first hired Mrs. Platt, a woman who had had experience running her

structure the appearance of strong kinship with its site on the hillside." The Manor as the Raouls, Gilbert and Parsons planned, was sited on the crown of a knoll that gently sloped down to Charlotte Street and offered spectacular views to the western mountains.

"All of the rooms at The Manor are front rooms. Those on the west and south open on a splendid view of the distant Blue Ridge Mountains with the broad, smooth roads and green lawns of Grove Park in the immediate foreground; while from the eastern rooms one looks out upon the attractive landscape of Albemarle Park, backed by the wooded

The Manor was an immediate success, prompting the addition, in 1903, of a large wing at the northern corner of the original building. This wing added two floors of additional guest rooms and a large, two-story ballroom that opened out onto the expansive front lawn.

own boarding house—the Van Gilder House on College Street—to manage the details of the Inn's operation.

"I have learned a good deal about running a hotel since I have been at this work and feel less and less confident that I would be successful if I had to deal with the details of the work. In the first place I do not think that I would be a success in the kitchen as I have never had very much experience about cooking and I think that I do not have the taste for so many of the delicate things that are required.

"I think that if we want to run a house such as The Manor has always been, that it will be much better to have a lady in charge as there are many duties that she could perform that a man could not. Just think how much the majority of our patrons are women and when they are sick how necessary it is to have a lady to minister to their wants.

"Then too I think the person in charge of the house should be in the house every night and be with the boarders to sit around and play cards with them, meet newcomers and talk to them and introduce them to the others, and be the social person of the house. I sup-

Suzy Saxon "at the chimes" in the lobby, about to ring in the afternoon meal for the guests in the adjacent sitting rooms.

The sitting room behind the main fireplace in the lobby, which looked out over the lawn at Charlotte Street.

The ladies' parlor, upstairs above the lobby sitting room, which featured a magnificent view of the mountain sunsets and, later, became part of "The Grace Kelly Suite."

The main sitting room, which was the original dining room for the guests, before the 1913 addition was built.

Peacock Alley, with its wicker rockers and writing tables, through which the elegantly dressed women "strutted" to supper.

DINING ROOM, THE NEW MANOR, ASHEVILLE, N.C.

The Manor dining room, added in 1913, enabled the Inn to serve up to a hundred guests at one time. Berkey & Gay, a leading furniture company working in the Arts & Crafts style in Grand Rapids, Michigan, supplied the tables and chairs.

pose I could do this but I know that it would mean giving up every other interest I had and doing that which is as different from my nature as white is from black. Unless I am willing to say good bye to the outside world and live a life entirely within the walls of The Manor I think I better keep my present relations in regard to the house." (Thomas Wadley Raoul to his mother, from Asheville, Feb. 7, 1900)

Mrs. Platt was the first of several managers that would work for Thomas, who was always, it seems, in search of the perfect corps of servants and staff to make The Manor the best place in Asheville.

"I have a man as a sort of a steward but I do all of the marketing, and I have no housekeeper but a head chambermaid. I decided to go through one season this way so that I would know more exactly what the duties of my manager were and I would know what to exact from them." (Thomas Wadley Raoul to his sister, Mary, from Albemarle Park, Jan. 14, 1902)

In 1903, when Thomas suffered a major relapse of his tuberculosis, John Burckel, William Greene Raoul's personal assistant, was sent down to manage the operations and complete the construction on the Clubhouse and the cottages that were underway. He remained after Thomas returned, and was succeeded by A. H. Malone, in the last years of the Raoul's involvement with The Manor. Gaston Raoul also spent time in Asheville helping oversee matters when Thomas needed assistance in the early years.

The Manor kitchen prided itself on the "distinctive southern cooking" it provided for the guests of The Inn and cottages.

Proof that Thomas found good staff who were loyal and devoted to serving the needs of The Manor is evidenced in a tribute printed in The Asheville Citizen on June 1, 1920 at the time he sold The Manor. In it are listed the names and years of service of the staff, some of whom had worked with him for nearly twenty years.

Thomas wrote regular weekly reports on the finances and the status of his guests to both of his parents and relied on their knowledge and advice in making the hard business decisions regarding the management of the place. He realized early on, however, that his best talents lay in the construction of and planning for the growth of Albemarle Park.

As The Manor succeeded, the pressure to grow out of the boarding house class increased. In 1903, he began construction of a new wing that extended out from the north end of the original building toward Charlotte Street. The large porch at the end of the first structure was removed to connect this addition. It continues in the Tudoresque style of the original wing, "appearing to float above the sloping lawn on a stuccoed base punctuated with semicircular arched doors and brick voussoirs," arches shaped to fit the curve. The

Thomas writing to his mother about the unique brick paving technique he developed to provide horses adequate footing on the steep hill up Terrace Road to the porte cochere at the entrance to The Manor.

most striking exterior feature of this wing is the massive brick chimney with its vertical detailing and the tall arched window centered in its face.

This new addition, containing two full floors of rooms and several other interesting interior spaces, greatly increased the Inn's capacity. The entire ground level was given over to a two-story ballroom.

With its arched proscenium stage and large windows it was the center of many social and theatrical events planned for the enjoyment of the guests as well as the general public. At the rear of the ballroom, a mezzanine offered an ideal vantage point for the performances below. Large double doors led to the expansive lawn that stretched down to Charlotte Street.

Hidden away behind the ballroom's stage, with its own private entrance from outside, and a narrow stairwell to the upstairs hallway, was the cozy, two room Honeymoon Suite, more private even than the individual cottages up the hill.

These improvements served The Manor well. In the letters he wrote his parents, Thomas continually related the numbers of guests he had at the Inn, often mentioning, with a measure of pride, how he had to turn away more guests due to the lack of accommodations.

By 1913, the year William Greene Raoul died, the many members of the Raoul family had begun to develop other interests.

Thomas began to concentrate on maximizing the profits from The Manor operation, to make it more attractive to potential buyers.

Aware that E.W. Grove's Grove Park Inn, less than a mile away, would soon begin to offer stiff competition for business, he decided to add a second wing to The Manor, to expand its capacity even more. This addition extended eastward from the original 1899 structure and elevated the Inn to the level of a first class hotel.

This wing has been characterized as "less picturesque" than the two previous wings, which can probably be ascribed to the absence of William Greene Raoul and Bradford Gilbert in its designing. While Thomas did not have the benefit of his father's architectural guidance, he still managed to capture many of the Tudoresque features of the earlier buildings.

The main dining room and enormous kitchen, which dominate the entire first floor, are the two most important features of this new wing. With their addition, The Manor could now easily accommodate seventy five to a hundred guests at a single sitting. Children were served their meals in another dining room reserved just for them, at the eastern end of the building.

Above the dining room are two floors of additional guest rooms and a third floor that was used to store the guests' extra luggage.

This wing also has an elevator, at one end of Peacock Alley near the dining room.

"Peacock Alley," angling away from the porte cochere along the curved entrance drive, connects this new wing to the original 1899 building at the corner of the lobby. This gallery was filled with light and served as a sun room and sitting room during the day, with wicker seats and writing tables lining both walls. As evening approached, the men would gather there, to "appreciate" the female guests who, dressed in all their finery, would pass through to the main dining room and the evening supper, "strutting like peacocks."

This dining room replaced the original, which was converted into additional sitting and game rooms. Several pairs of french

— 36 —

The Manor Inn after the 1913 wing was built. The brick paving on Terrace Road next to Clover cottage is visible in the foreground (ca. 1921).

The 1913 wing with its large open porch just off the main dining room.

doors open out from the dining room onto a long covered porch that looks out upon the main entry drive.

An octagonal room known as "The Hunt Room" was located along the north side of the Inn, straddling the service drive, and was yet another of the many public rooms provided for the use of the guests. When a group of Chinese visitors stayed at The Manor, two ping pong tables were moved into this room and the days were filled with the clamor of tournament play.

The Manor Inn, finally complete in the mind of the Raouls, continued to enjoy great success and, together with the Cottages, was one of the premier hotels in Asheville even after The Grove Park Inn was opened. It remained profitable for many more years and was operated year-round, rather than seasonally, as was the case with the Grove Park Inn.

The Raouls' vision of "an English Inn in America" still stands today, the sole remnant from Asheville's boom period during the late 1800s, when the Battery Park Hotel, the Kenilworth Inn, the Swannanoa Hotel and many other elegant resorts served an eclectic array of visitors from around the world.

The view from Cherokee cottage, ca. 1921, looking out over The Manor and Clover cottage to the western mountains. Several guests returning from a pleasant horse ride can be seen coming up Cherokee Road from the entrance at the Lodge.

Looking out onto Charlotte Street through the archway at the Lodge, colorfully embraced by flowering vines of running rose.

The Landscape of Albemarle Park: Samuel Parsons' Vision

Charles A. Birnbaum, ASLA

Background

Samuel Parsons, Jr., the landscape architect for Albemarle Park.

"Its treatment need not be surprisingly original, or fanciful, or picturesque, but there should be sane consideration of all aspects practical and aesthetic, of the possibilities of the case, as will secure that sort of perfect relation of all its parts which will give it a dignified and sensible beauty that, if it does not surprise at first, will charm after all, and will *last*." (Samuel Parsons, Jr.) [1]

Samuel Parsons, Jr. was working in partnership with George F. Pentecost, Jr. when, in the late 1880s, he developed the plan for Albemarle Park for a challenging site in the mountains of western North Carolina. At the time Parsons undertook this commission he was an established leader in the development of the profession of landscape architecture.

Born Feb. 7, 1844, in New Bedford, Massachusetts, Samuel Parsons, Jr. was third in a line of Quaker horticulturists. The Parsons family members were descendants of nurserymen that had been propagating and cultivating nursery stock for more than two centuries.

In 1840, Parsons' grandfather established a nursery for his sons, Samuel Baum Parsons and his two brothers, in Flushing, New York.

It was quite prosperous, and brought the Parsons family an international reputation that led to extensive travel abroad. This gave them unique opportunities to introduce new ornamental trees and shrubs in the United States and meet with individuals who were showing great promise in the emerging field of landscape architecture.

As a youth, Parsons worked as an apprentice in the family business. Yearning to satisfy "the study of nature that had been [his] delight from boyhood" [2] he continued his education in related sciences at the Flushing Institute, followed by three years at Haverford College. In 1860, he entered the Sheffield Scientific School at Yale College with a major course emphasis in agricultural chemistry.

Following these studies, Parsons kept an interest in the family nursery for two to three years, eventually purchasing a farm in New Jersey where he resided for six years. During this time, Parsons' name and his family's reputation enabled him to secure commissions which drew on his vast horticultural knowledge. He yearned, however, to understand more about the practice of landscape design and pursued an association with Calvert Vaux, whom he ultimately looked

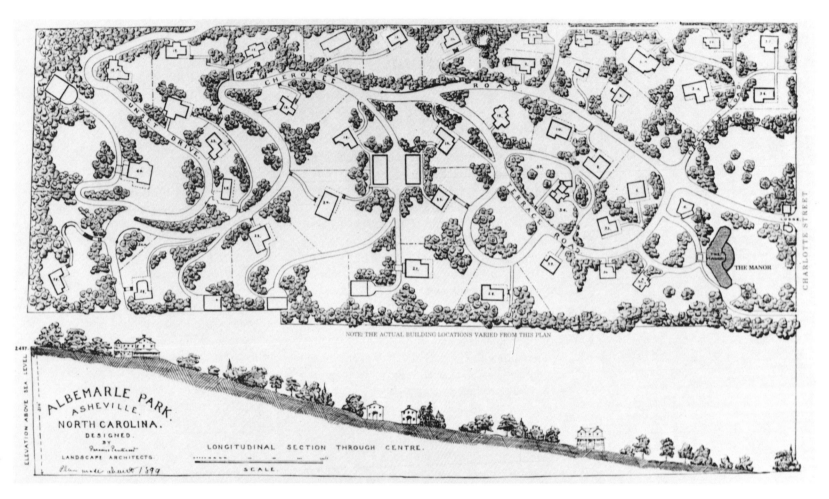

NOTE: THE ACTUAL BUILDING LOCATIONS VARIED FROM THIS PLAN

upon as "a special guide, philosopher and friend." [3] In 1880, he seized the opportunity to join Calvert Vaux as a partner in Vaux and Co. in New York City. Vaux's reputation was well established and, when he was offered the position as New York City's Landscape Architect with the Department of Parks, he declined to serve alone, choosing only to accept the position when it was agreed that the entire firm, Vaux and Company, which included Parsons, would be hired. Parsons then went on to serve as the Superintendent of Planting which, in his words, was "actually Mr. Vaux's assistant." [4] During this time, Parsons assisted Vaux in carrying out and perfecting many plans for Central Park, other parks across the city and private commissions. His keen knowledge of plant materials complemented Vaux's skills and overall design philosophy and intent. This is most clearly illustrated in their earliest joint publi-

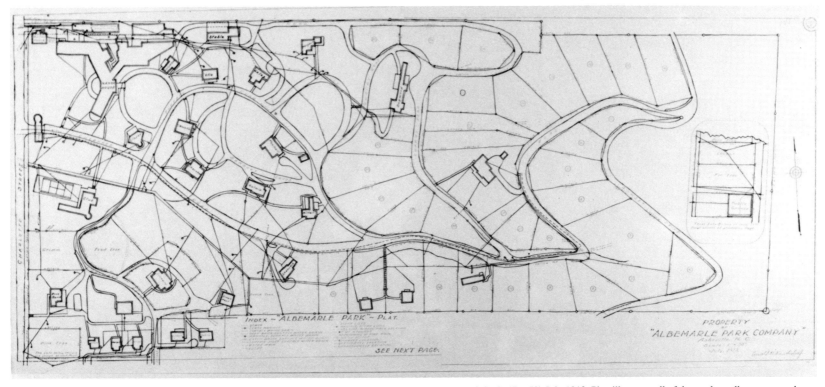

The As-Built Plan, titled "Property of Albemarle Park Company, Asheville, N.C." Signed Arnold H. Vanderhoof, Scale 1" = 50', July 1913. Plan illustrates all of the roads, walks, steps, swales and utilities.

Left: The Schematic Design Plan, titled, "Albemarle Park, Asheville, North Carolina. Designed by Parsons & Pentecost Landscape Architects", ca. 1890s.

cation, Concerning Lawn Planting in 1881, an essay prepared to "advance the standard of landscape architecture in the United States."[5]

Parsons continued his service with the New York City Parks Department as the city's landscape architect from Vaux's death in 1895 until his retirement in 1911. He implemented the schematic designs by Vaux and Frederick Law Olmsted for large picturesque parks, and the designs that were conceived in collaboration with Vaux for the smaller parks, usually under ten acres in size.

He supplemented this work with projects he conceived, including many small and medium picturesque and reform era parks and playgrounds. He served as the city's landscape architect during a period of enormous expansion and stewardship, orchestrating the efforts of both department staff and nationally significant design consultants.[6]

During his tenure Parsons worked diligently to acquire land in the most crowded tenement districts for urban green "breathing spaces"[7] such as Thomas Jefferson and

A bird's eye view of Albemarle Park, ca. 1905, looking northwest from a hill southeast of Crow's Nest, visible in the lower left corner. Shamrock and Milfoil cottages are in the center and right foreground. In the background, l to r, are The Manor Inn, Clover, Cherokee, Clematis, Columbus, Clio, and Galax cottages. The line of evenly spaced green ash trees can be seen along the edge of Cherokee Road above the open greensward below Crow's Nest.

DeWitt Clinton Parks which still survive today.

One of his best remembered contributions was his protection of the naturalistic design of the parks that were under his supervision. He opposed the privatization of public parks, and prevented the construction of racetracks, menageries and other public exhibition spaces within park boundaries.

In addition to this commitment as a public servant, he wrote prolifically on issues of landscape design and horticulture, and published numerous articles and several books.

Among his noteworthy landscapes are St. Nicolas and Seward Parks in New York City, The Mall in Washington, D.C, and campus plans for Colorado College, Princeton University and many others.

Although, in 1991, Samuel Parsons, Jr. does not share the same name recognition as, say, Frederick Law Olmsted, his diverse legacy of extant landscapes, spread over seventeen states, is well known and much beloved. At the time of Parsons' death in 1923, James Greenleaf, then President of the American Society of Landscape Architects, the organization that was founded in Parsons' office 25 years earlier, stated that "It is quite possible to some the name and influence of Samuel Parsons may seem remote, so rapidly does the hand of time blur our impressions, but those who knew him do not forget and his name is permanently inscribed with honour upon our records."[8]

Parsons' legacy of residential park design, to which he devoted an entire chapter in his volume How to Plan the Home Grounds, has not been forgotten and is very

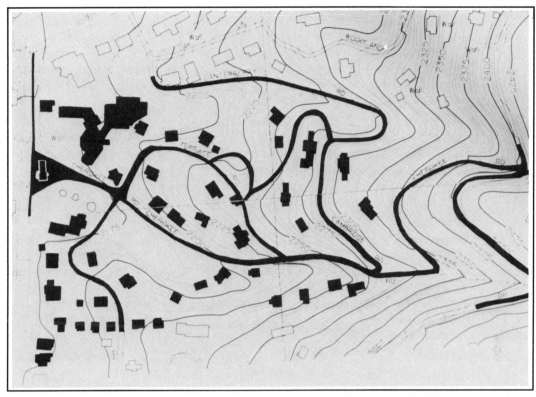

Photogrametric Map by L. Robert Kimball & Associates, April 1985. Scale 1" = 200'. Roads and buildings have been highlighted to illustrate their integration with topography.

much intact and vital in Albemarle Park in Asheville, North Carolina.

For this forty-two acre site Parsons applied many of the principles he had perfected over the previous two decades, acquired from his experiences in the planning of public parks, cemeteries, residential plots and country places around the country. He approached Albemarle Park with an enthusiastic sensitivity to the site's natural beauty and worked to ensure that the overall effect be picturesque and provide each individual lot with a "miniature park."[9]

Parsons was able, through the use of proven landscape design principles and site-sensitive, innovative engineering practices, to meet the functional, aesthetic and economic

Looking east up Cherokee Road at Milfoil (left) and Shamrock cottages. The stone retaining wall is visible along the upper right edge of Cherokee Road. A wooden footbridge provided access across the landscaped gully to Brown Bear and Wildfell cottages.

Approaching the Landscape and Developing the Scheme

"There should be a general scheme from which everything naturally develops in its relative and just order and place, and the basis of all design and of all arrangements should be the natural conformation and incidents of the ground." (Samuel Parsons, Jr.)[11]

Samuel Parsons found the site to be a challenge, offering him opportunities to sympathetically respect and enhance its rugged terrain, sweeping vistas, native stands of trees and woodland vegetation. He said that it may not have been the most perfect, but, like the architect Bradford Gilbert, he was "very enthusiastic about the place."[12]

When he initially approached the site, which was "half covered" with a "fine forest of chestnut and oaks," he recognized that the existing landscape must control the general design.[13] He acknowledged that it must never endanger or discomfort the resident by "shutting out" or limiting sunlight or air, or otherwise create unhealthy and uncomfortable conditions with areas of low, damp ground or bleak exposure.

Parsons states that "there are certain primary conditions or divisions that make up all residential or public parks." Walks, drives, greenswards or lawns, plantations—whether trees, shrubs, or flowers, and the intermediate spaces that may be called "sloping grounds"—all these make up characteristic

requirements of his clients.

Today, Albemarle Park remains an enduring product of Parsons' vision, retaining much of his original intent. It provides us with an important glimpse back into the practice of landscape architecture during the last quarter of the 19th century, a period when significant achievements were made in the planning and design of residential parks.

It seems fitting that Samuel Parsons Jr. should lay out this site concurrent with the founding of the American Society of Landscape Architects (ASLA) in 1899.

During the initial ASLA meetings, many of which were held at the office of Parsons & Pentecost, Parsons played a major role, serving as the chair of the committee that developed the Constitution. This document describes the landscape architect as one who "practices the art of arranging land and landscape for use and enjoyment." Parsons' role at Albemarle Park could not be described more fittingly.[10]

"landscape-gardening effects."

Today we refer to these landscape elements as character defining features.

Samuel Parsons sought to embrace these features through the careful arrangement of drives, walks, residences, furnishings and a site-specific palette of plant materials and "plantations." This comprehensive approach to community planning had been successfully achieved as early as 1853 in the United States by Andrew Jackson Davis in Llewellyn Park, West Orange, New Jersey, and by Frederick Law Olmsted, Sr. and Calvert Vaux, in projects such as Parkside, Buffalo, and Riverside, Illinois.

Albemarle Park was a ground-breaking achievement of its time due to Parsons' successful manipulation of a site with slopes that averaged a twenty per-cent gradient.

Parsons referred to this type of residential community as a "Homestead Park". Much of Albemarle Park is still a vibrant and thriving community today, true to Parsons' ideal and testimony to the manner in which it was originally laid out, recognizing that "art and beauty in such cases always goes hand in hand with common sense and reasonable comfort." [14]

Postcard view of Chipmunk Cottage from The Circle. Foreground planting includes a lush carpet of ground cover along its steep slope, informally placed oaks, dogwoods and shrubs of rhodedendron and native azalea. Ca. 1920s.

The Albemarle Park Landscape

A rich and diverse collection of historic plans, photographs, post cards and other items still exists that allows us to develop an understanding of the divisions of the Albemarle Park landscape.

Two historic plans that survived enable us to examine the designer's intent and compare it with what was actually executed at Albemarle Park. These are the Parsons & Pentecost schematic design plan with a longitudinal section for Albemarle Park, ca. 1899, and a plat titled Property of "Albemarle Park Company", dated July 1913.

When the two plans are overlaid, it is clear how closely the original scheme was followed by the Raoul family when Albemarle Park's parcels were sold and "built out." These plans, along with the other images and descriptions, allow us to divide the landscape composition into discrete divisions.

Postcard view of the entrance to Clematis Cottage including the prolific Michigan Running Prairie Rose, Rosa setigera, which Parsons considered ideal for this hillside territory, ca. 1910.

Landscape Composition and Plant Materials

"Our first duty is to frankly preserve, without attempting to imitate the existing beauties of the place—woodlands, single trees, rocks, knolls, and meadows—and to only add such arrangements of trees and shrubs and flowers as will enhance and perfect the special charms that are native to the place, and at the same time not interfere with the comfort and convenience of the people who live there." (Samuel Parsons, Jr.) [15]

Historically, the landscape palette at Albemarle was extremely diverse ranging from broad native woodlands, free standing "plantations", bank plantings of shrubs and groundcovers, meadows, manicured lawns and limited herbaceous plantings. Upon review of the design plan it is clear that every effort was made to maintain the native woodlands when possible.

Today, many of the original deciduous and conifer trees remain, though some of the diversity of the understory planting is lost.

Parsons' intent for these home grounds was for the visitor to view its rich and diverse landscape as a whole. The steep grades provide a variety of overlooks from where one can see "great groves of trees intermingled with shrubs, and vines". Parsons understood how plants should be clustered, arranged and cultivated so that they would remain vigorous for years and require "little pruning, trans-

Clover cottage, viewed from the lawn beside the Clubhouse tennis courts.

planting, or other change." These landscapes features, he said, should "be managed so as to make us think of the most charming effects of woodland and meadow, and yet not for a moment deceive us, but make us, instead, exclaim how well the grouping is contrived for the open meadows and lawns and long vistas of the place, and at the same time for the individual exhibition of the native charms of the trees and shrubs." [16]

Examining the landscape composition of Albemarle Park from the most dense to the most open, one can note a direct relationship between density and maintenance.

First and foremost, Parsons was against any human intervention in the woodland

Parsons made great use of native plants, like this large stand of dogwood trees at the edge of a lawn, in his landscape design for Albemarle Park.

areas. The only exception would be "to encourage them and keep them growing in the most satisfactory way, and to leave them absolutely untouched by horticultural skills except that which undertakes to remove excrescences, superfluous branches, dead wood, and clogging pools of water."

He discouraged the introduction of maples and chestnuts along the perimeter edges of native groupings, fearing that intervention could "injure the native woodland effect, which is so easy to lose and hard to restore." [17]

He favored a treatment that was much softer for these native stands, based on his experiences as the Landscape Architect for New York City's Department of Parks. As in many of the larger natural parks, woodlands bordered on broad meadows. The results were charming parklike effects—where "nature has been just enough influenced by the hand of man to give her the human interest that should be associated with all attempts of the landscape gardener." [18]

The second greatest area of vegetative cover, following the woodland areas, could be found in the rich massing of irregular and regular groupings called "plantations". Many of these areas were preexisting, predominantly composed of canopy deciduous trees embellished with shrubs and vines.

The priority here was that new plantings emphasized "the open air comfort that is needed for each and all of the houses." Parsons viewed this dense enhancement of the plantation areas as the site's "crowning improvement". He suggested the use of a variety of vines and creepers, recommending these especially along roads, over rocks, and along steep banks for aesthetic reasons and to stabilize the extremely steep slopes "where a goat could hardly climb." [19]

Parsons used vines prolifically and found them to be "harmonious" with the "rugged character" of the preexisting landscape. A palette of creepers was developed and placed one to two feet apart in an irregular fashion. These carpet-like plants were highly invasive and quick to achieve a visual and functional impact.

Plant materials by genus and species are suggested in his writings, and include honeysuckle, running roses, wisteria frutescens, English ivy and the Michigan running prairie-rose (Rosa setigera). Of all the creepers, Parsons felt the prairie rose was "best suited for this hillside territory." [20]

To accompany the "plantation" treatment along the interior roads, Parsons recommended a limited number of free-standing trees to "temper the rays of the sun." These trees, with the exception of the evenly-spaced Ash trees along Cherokee Road, were irregularly planted or individually placed, like the understory palette of the plantation areas, though not accompanied by an integration of understory materials.

These areas of dappled shade were meant to provide shelter in specific locations and were placed, on the average "every forty or fifty feet" on center. To achieve this effect, Parsons recommended the use of mainly native species including: American ashes (Fraxinus americana), Tulip trees (Liriodendron tulipifera), American Lindens (Tilia americana), Pin Oaks (Quercus palustris), Chestnut-leaved Oaks (Quercus prinus), Wild Cherries, Norway Maples (Acer platanoides), Sugar Maples (Acer saccharinum), and Oriental Plane Trees (Platanus orientalis).[21] Many of these plantings still exist today and are of considerable size and caliper.

One of the most dramatic placements of informally standing trees in an open greensward park at The Circle. This slightly bowled, centrally located area contained "a few small oaks trees...but the beauty of the spot (was) specially improved by an undergrowth of vines and creeping evergreen plants, and the introduction of a noteworthy collection of the splendid native American azaleas: azalea calendulacea, azalea vaseyii, and azalea viscosa, some of which glow in

May and June with the most splendid tints of orange and red." This marriage of informally grouped oaks, dogwoods and hemlocks in an open lawn, with rhododendrons and azaleas along the edge, is unique to Albemarle Park, but extremely representative of much of the estate work that Parsons would execute over the next two decades.[22]

In addition to the unusual shrub treatment that embraces and encloses the outer edge of The Circle, Parsons also recommended shrub massing for the steepest and most rugged parts of the landscape that would provide a seasonal variation of blooms, in color, size and timing. It was in these areas, too steep for housing development, that a varied mix of understory shrubs was recommended. This included: Upright Honeysuckle (Lonicera fragrantissima), Spiraea (Spiraea opulifolia), Fortune's Forsythia (Forsythia fortunii) and Weeping Forsythia (Forsythia suspensa), Virginia Sweetspire (Itea virginica), Snowberry (Symphoricarpos glomerata), Mock orange (Philadelphus grandiflorus), Red-twigged dogwood (Cornus alba sanguinea), Chinese Privet (Ligustrum sinensis), Japan Eleagnus (Eleagnus angustifoloa), and Japan Barberry (Berberis japonicum).[23]

Parsons chose to mass significant quantities of the same genus of these understory plantings together, rather than intersperse and/or cluster a variety of species.

In addition to the common landscape types described above, there are several unique areas of Albemarle Park.

Transitional areas that were considered

Postcard view of the wisteria draped south porch of The Manor, overlooking Cherokee Road, ca. 1910.

"semi-public," those areas between and within the individual lots and along Albemarle's perimeter boundaries, were specifically addressed in Parsons' writings.

He felt that, within the lots themselves, "a few trees and shrubs, as well as vines [should be] planted in harmony with the gen-

Rosebank Cottage, Albemarle Park, Wichuriana Roses in bloom.
ASHEVILLE, N. C.

Rosebank cottage, viewed from Charlotte Street, ca. 1910. In the 1960s, the stone steps of Hillside Walk were relocated to the southern edge of the lot (to the right in the photo), the rose-covered bank was severely cut back and a two-tiered stone retaining wall was built in order to provide building space for a small commercial structure facing Charlotte Street. The building was never built.

eral system, so as to establish a certain standard of planting." He went on to recommend that such a treatment is desirable, not only in the short term, but should be "kept up in the future by all those who buy lots on which to construct homes."[24]

For areas between individual properties, Parsons favored a soft, natural vegetative buffer over the more architectonic solution. He suggests that "...three trees and a dozen shrubs of the right kind, and rightly arranged, will

make, in their way, as satisfactory and agreeable a screen for the hard lines of the fence or stone wall, as if they were replaced by a bordering of shrubs and trees a mile long."[25]

He encouraged a soft solution of naturalistic materials at all times instead of one that clearly illustrated human intervention.

Around the perimeter of the property, Parsons attempted to reinforce the regional, natural scenery with a vegetative edge that was sympathetic with the landscape composition

of Albemarle Park. For this area he suggested that "the entire exterior boundary of the place [have] a stout wire fence, covered with honeysuckles and Virginia creepers, and wherever trees and shrubs are lacking, care [be] taken to fill in" with harmonious materials.[26]

Parsons was opposed to the introduction of brightly colored ornamental trees and shrubs, especially in areas highly visible to the public. He recommended that the application of popular nursery stock such as Japanese maples (Acer japonicum), Purple Beeches (Fagus sylvatica 'Purpurea'), and Golden Oaks (Quercus) be avoided.

He encouraged all to show restraint when contemplating such additions and to use, instead, materials with a color scheme possessing "green tones."[27] Not to be totally disagreeable, Parsons recognized that in some cases personal taste would be followed. But in these situations, when the proposal is not in the overall spirit of the grounds, it should be delegated to an area within the individual homeowner's lot that is not visible to those outside. He goes on to state that "nothing was permitted that would tend to destroy the natural woodland effect."[28]

Early photographic views illustrate applications of the type of treatment Parsons favored for herbaceous materials including the clustering of small colonies of same-genus plant materials, "particularly wild-looking flowers" such as Asters (Asteramellus) and Daisies (Michaelmas). This would be most successful when placed on the transitional perimeters of woodlands, where they meet open lawns and

Kalmia Cottage, Albemarle Park
Asheville, N. C.

Kalmia cottage, framed with vines, as viewed from Cherokee Road, ca. 1914.

Panoramic postcard view of the Albemarle landscape "plantation" planting surrounding Fox Hall, Clematis and Cherokee cottages with mountainous woodland backdrop, ca. 1910.

Postcard view from Cherokee Road looking west toward the Lodge. Note the locust post "bollards" that establish a virtual edge on the left hand side of the road. In the 1950s the entrance road was reconfigured to go around the Lodge, a parking area was cut into the lawn and three rondettes were located there.

meadows and "sunlight might reach them..." [29]

The landscape Parsons recommended for Albemarle Park was both rich and diverse, yet harmonious with its native surroundings. The other landscape divisions discussed below were always well integrated with this lush, vegetative palette.

The ability to understand the aesthetic, physical and functional qualities of these plants was probably one of the greatest skills of this third generation horticulturist.

Roads and Paths

"Roads and paths are the dumb conductors of the visitor and should serve in themselves to guide him easily towards every spot which could afford enjoyment. Roads and paths, therefore, should not be too conspicuous but should be carefully laid out and concealed by plantations." (Samuel Parsons, Jr.) [30]

Postcard view of Orchard Road, ca. 1910, showing the turret at the corner of the Clubhouse where the ladies awaited their turn to bowl. The brick drainage swales are also evident.

A review of the original design scheme for Albemarle Park and the existing circulation patterns today will reveal roads of "almost spiral curves." [31] For most of their lengths these drives are quite gracious, but, at their turning points, they appear to switch-back onto themselves in an effort to overcome the site's steep grades, and to provide panoramic views. Roads are well integrated and are buffered from adjacent residences or other roads in close proximity by the naturally steep slopes that were heavily planted. This primary circulation network was originally coupled with a limited number of narrow walks, about four feet wide, which generally connected individual residences to their closest access road. Interior paths connecting individual units or other destinations were employed only by necessity. Integral with these walks, "occasional hillside flights of steps (were) introduced, to reach house sites that a carriage may not attempt to approach." [32]

The roads of Albemarle Park were designed with a maximum "a fourteen per cent grade, over which it is possible for a carriage to pass with some degree of comfort." [33] These roads were not likely heavily travelled, accommodating only vehicles and pedestrians that wished to visit neighboring cottages.

Parsons viewed roads and paths as "necessary evils that add no landscape beauty to the place." His limited application of such hard surfaces in the schematic design plan for Albemarle Park reinforces his simple "toleration" for such functional pedestrian amenities.

It is also evident in these early views that great efforts were made to "minimize their essential ugliness, and to contrive how to manage with so few of them as possible." This

Current view of the eastern entrance into Albemarle Park from Cherokee Road, with Sunset Drive above, illustrates the topographical manipulation that was required to integrate a comprehensive circulation system.

crushing and the paving of the roads. Although the road has been resurfaced with asphalt several times over, many of the stone curbs and gutters can be identified today.

Topographic Variation: Sloping Ground

"The unusual feature of the place is its steepness. The natural contours in many places will hardly allow one to reach its upper portions without the most strenuous effort." (Samuel Parsons, Jr.) [35]

Parsons recognized that it would have been much easier to select a level or rolling piece of ground, with grades reasonably easy and "the course of the roads and the shape of the lots so much more readily adapted to the ends of design."[36] He understood, however, that this site would afford spectacular views and, therefore, took full advantage of this unique opportunity. In both Albemarle Park in the mid to late 1890s and the more gardenesque Mountain Terrace in Birmingham, Alabama in the early 1900s, Parsons mastered the manipulation of steep topography.

The results of this sympathetic intervention were broad scenic panoramas for pedestrians and residents, generous quantities of natural light achieved through selective thinning, and a comfortable separation between pedestrians and vehicles. This unique ability to take advantage of severe grades is a direct result of his experience with the rugged landscapes of Morningside, Riverside and upper

manipulation and minimization he viewed as "the duty of the landscape architect".[34]

Finally, Parsons believed that the construction of such circulation systems should be aesthetically pleasing, but should also be built to last. The original construction material was a macadam foundation with gravel surface. Such a treatment was typical of the era and was commonly used in many city parks and country places. A detailed specification for the construction of such roads was pub-

lished as an Appendix in Parsons' How to Plan the Home Grounds. This costly, enduring treatment included solid stone gutters and a detailed drainage system with integrated drainage inlets. The Raoul sons, schooled in engineering both at the university and on their father's railroad, did much of the work that was necessary to implement Samuel Parsons' plan. They surveyed the property, oversaw the laying of the excellent drainage system throughout the site and supervised the rock

An early photo of the Lodge as viewed from Cherokee Road clearly shows an example of brick swales that were used throughout Albemarle Park.

Central parks in New York City.

The grades at Albemarle Park on the average measure a slope of over twenty per cent—"a rise of one foot for every five feet of longitudinal extent." Therefore, one end of this forty acre property is 300 feet higher than the other. To complicate the situation further, Parsons noted that "the contours are strongly plicated laterally, so that a backbone or ridge runs right up through the center, with deeply depressed valleys on either side."

Although these depressed valleys have recently had their streams rechannelled and diverted into culverts below grade, overall the remaining topographic features are intact and are one of the greatest character defining features of the landscape.

As was the case historically, the natural landforms should be preserved and stabilized where necessary to insure their longevity and to protect them from "washing," which could result in "deeply scored hollows and uneven depressions." [37]

"A Class of Structures"

"There are, however, a class of structures, thoroughly architectural in their character, but having such close sympathy with their environment that it is easy to feel that they belong to the landscape in a more intimate way than, for example, house and stables." (Samuel Parsons, Jr.)[38]

"Closely-Massed Rocks on Finished Steep Bank" from Landscape Gardening, by Samuel Parsons, 1891.

Contemporary photograph of wall of naturally grouped boulders along Banbury Cross covered by cascading English ivy.

Beginning with the picturesque cottages whose style was suggested by the "ruggedness of the grounds," [39] there is an overall design vocabulary of structures and furnishings which display a hierarchy similar to that of the "soft" or natural landscape features.

Cottages

The individual cottages were sited on lots that ranged from one-half to three acres, and were "in each case carefully studied with the architect (Bradford Gilbert) in the original plan."[40] In most cases, the cottages had been sited so that they appear to come down the drives or walks, or slope upward in steps to higher plateaus or terraces upon which the individual residences are placed. This treatment, when combined with the rich variety of planting, never reveals more than a portion of three or four residences from any one location.

As illustrated in the historic photographs and the 1913 survey, the nineteen original shingle-style structures were carefully integrated with their landscape surrounds. They were aptly titled with such plant names as Clover, Clematis, Dogwood, Orchard, Shamrock, Rose Bank, Kalmia, Dahlia and Daffodil, further illustrating the premier importance of the landscape.

Walls

"...We believe that if they learned how to design the form and coloring of the wall better, and too ornament its surface with suitable vines, we would not hear so much about making lawns without wall or fence." (Samuel Parsons, Jr.) [41]

Postcard view titled, "One of the pretty little cottages in connection with 'The Manor', Albemarle Park, Asheville, N.C.", ca. 1910. Note the perimeter fence in the foreground of locust posts joined by two rows of horizontal wire members.

In addition to the cottages, the appropriate use of site furnishings has also been addressed in Parsons' writings. Linear elements such as fences and walls were the preferred choice of the period wherever boundary lines were established. Recognizing the need for this programmatic requirement, Parsons urged that the "landscape would be almost invariably improved if we could eliminate the wall or fence altogether, for, as with roads and paths, the landscape would be better without than with them." [42]

However, recognizing that walls would be used, and since, sometimes, the steep grades actually warranted their application, the compromise Parsons suggested was that when walls were to be sited, the "length to which they are extended may be, by exercise of ingenuity, limited to the shortest possible distance, and the design of the wall constructed may be greatly developed and improved in the direction of agreeable lines and masses of color; and, further, its objectionable character may be greatly suppressed by sinking or screening it, allowing the eye to pass over it, as in the case of the so-called ha-ha fence." [43]

Many walls still exist today and are part of a vocabulary of native stone that includes retaining walls, free standing walls, stairs, bridges and culverts. These built features were applied to arrest the steeply graded slope or to allow for pedestrian or vehicular circulation; they were not applied to privatize or screen one residence from another.

Parsons used this vocabulary in many of his commissions. He recognized the value of a stone or brick wall which in many situations had a rounded, or "graceful" cap, and a top line. He felt that the surface of such elements should allow for an attractive amount of light and shade, produced by designed recesses or roughness in the material used, and, it should be clad with English ivy, or, better still, by Japanese ivy, to give it a "charming character."

He also noted that these plant materials should not be mingled with Virginia creepers or roses setigera and wichuriana." [44]

Fences

"...Fences are an advantage to the place only so far as they afford the seclusion and protection from without. They are less defensible than walls, because they can hardly be made altogether satisfactory in line, contour, or surface; therefore, what we can do with fences to render them tolerable is to either make them a solid barrier of close-growing vines, or to construct them of wires which, at a little distance, are entirely visible." (Samuel Parsons, Jr.) [45]

Although Parsons clearly states his attitude toward fences here, a limited application of fences and fence posts can be found in the photographic record at Albemarle. The most consistent applications are the "stout wire fence" that was used around the perimeter and was visually screened by the lush vegetation in these buffer areas, and the use of locust posts in common areas as bollards that are visible in many of the historic images. The locust post also served as the standard post for free standing street signs and lights.

Photographs of the few detached fences used in Albemarle Park show that they were quite low, usually two to three feet in height. They appear to be constructed of vertical locust post members which support two horizontal wires. This fence clearly denotes a private front yard, but it does not shatter the landscape composition - the wire is so light that it is difficult to see unless one is quite close.

Although privacy fences, such as the picket fence that was popular at this time, were found in other neighborhoods in Asheville, they were discouraged here and viewed "in all its forms of both iron and wood, [as] a contrivance that tends to produce a disagreeable effect, because its upright bars are apt to multiply and confuse the detached glimmers of view we get through the regularly intermittent open spaces." [46]

"Rock-work"

"One rock in the wrong place, looking as if it had fallen unawares out of a cart, is totally out of place, while a number of rocks, spotted about in quite promiscuous fashion at the base of a slope abounding in large and small masses of stone, will often help the beauty of the landscape, especially if a footpath is present that appears to be here and there deflected by the presence of the rock." (Samuel Parsons, Jr.) [47]

One of the most subtle features of the original Albemarle Park landscape was the informal placement of rocks. These native stones which were probably unearthed during the initial excavation for the drainage system and the cottages, were originally "grouped and massed with the utmost taste and discretion." Parsons stressed that if this placement was not sensitively executed, the result would otherwise mar the landscape.[48]

Parsons wrote of five opportunities for the placement of rocks whose effect should always "look natural." These include: a bank treatment

Embellishments such as this light fixture luminaire standard were part of the original design and were similar to those used in Biltmore Village. One still exists today near Crow's Nest cottage.

with rocks, groups of stones placed to protect an important tree, at the curves of drives to fend off carriage wheels, along extended terraces, and in front, or at the side of the cottage.

He wrote of these broad policies in 1898, in <u>Landscape Gardening</u>, concurrent with his

The upper entrance to the Clubhouse, as viewed from Cherokee Road. Rustic twig benches sit on the lawn near the tennis courts.

The historic photographic record does, however, include examples of lights and signs that were harmonious with the landscape. One of the historic views shows a rustic bench that is reminiscent of those in Central Park.

One can only speculate that Parsons would not have approved of more ornamental embellishments such as statuary, urns, and sundials, since he states that, regarding a natural landscape's perimeter wall, this barrier "should have a simple unobtrusive character...and to preserve the character no special ornaments such as statues or urns." [51]

Conclusion

Albemarle Park is the unified vision of a proprietor, landscape architect, architect and engineer. It utilized what were, for its time, premier principles in the planning, laying out and engineering of residential parks. It combined state of the art construction methodologies and the use of enduring natural and constructed materials.

Samuel Parsons' visionary design for Albemarle Park embraced the entire spectrum of the natural landscape features of the site: its rugged terrain, watersheds, native plant materials, and excellent viewshed opportunities.

The result of this sympathetic manipulation by a master designer and knowledgeable horticulturalist is a homestead park that, on the eve of its centennial, is still true to the original design intent, still substantially intact, and still recognized by the people who live there and come to visit as a very special place.

work at Albemarle Park.[49]

The successful placement and integration of rocks into the landscape was not new to Parsons. Early photographs of Central and Morningside parks in New York City that were executed under Parsons as the city's Landscape Architect illustrate a similar intent to the one intended for Albemarle. In all of these cases the placement of rocks has a "definite fundamental scheme, springing naturally from the shape of the ground and nature of its rocky contents, and that the carrying out of this scheme had best be done in a large and bold fashion." [50]

Embellishments

Parsons does not address ornamental embellishments or furnishings such as signs, lights, benches, planters, urns or statuary for Albemarle Park or other natural landscapes.

Notes

1. Samuel Parsons Jr, <u>How to Plan the Home Grounds,</u> (New York, Doubleday & McClure Co. 1899), p. 184.
2. <u>Memories of Samuel Parsons</u>, Edited by Mabel Parsons, C.P. Putnam's Sons, New York and London, 1926, p.3
3. Ibid, p.9.
4. Ibid, p. 10.
5. <u>Concerning Lawn Planting</u>, Calvert Vaux and Samuel Parsons, Jr., Orange Judd Company, New York, 1881.
6. This determination was made in part by the collection of representative projects in the Central Park Collection at the Municipal Archives, New York City, New York.
7. Garden and Forest, June 05, 1895, p.222
8. Letter from James Greenleaf to Mabel Parsons, 1926, Samuel Parsons, Jr. file, Long Island Room, Queens Library.
9. Samuel Parsons, Jr. <u>Landscape Gardening Studies</u>, (John Lane Company, New York, 1910) p.33.
10. <u>Landscape Gardening Studies</u>, p.10.
11. <u>How to Plan the Home Grounds</u>, p. viii.
12. Letter from Thomas Wadley Raoul to his Mother from the Battery Park Hotel, Asheville, North Carolina, September 4, 1897.
13. <u>How to Plan the Home Grounds</u>, p. 177.
14. <u>How to Plan the Home Grounds</u>, p. viii.
15. <u>How to Plan the Home Grounds</u>, p. 164.
16. <u>How to Plan the Home Grounds</u>, p. 163.
17. Ibid.
18. <u>How to Plan the Home Grounds</u>, p. 162.
19. <u>How to Plan the Home Grounds</u>, p. 179.
20. <u>How to Plan the Home Grounds</u>, p. 180.
21. Ibid.
22. <u>How to Plan the Home Grounds</u>, p. 182.
23. <u>How to Plan the Home Grounds</u>, p. 179.
24. <u>How to Plan the Home Grounds</u>, pp. 170-71.
25. <u>How to Plan the Home Grounds</u>, p. 189.
26. <u>How to Plan the Home Grounds</u>, pp. 181-82.
27. Samuel Parsons, Jr., <u>Landscape Gardening</u>, (G.P. Putnam's Sons, New York, London, 1891), p. xvi.*
28. <u>Landscape Gardening Studies</u>, p.35.
29. <u>How to Plan the Home Grounds</u>, p. 160.
30. Samuel Parsons, <u>The Art of Landscape Architecture In Development and its Application to Modern Landscape Gardening</u>, (G.P. Putnam's Sons New York and London, The Knickerbocker Press, 1915), p. 132.
31. <u>Landscape Gardening Studies</u>, p. 34.
32. <u>How to Plan the Home Grounds</u>, p. 178.
33. <u>How to Plan the Home Grounds</u>, p. 177.
34. <u>Landscape Gardening</u>, p. xv.
35. <u>Landscape Gardening Studies</u>, p. 34.
36. <u>How to Plan the Home Grounds</u>, p. 176.
37. <u>Landscape Gardening Studies</u>, p. 35.
38. <u>How to Plan the Home Grounds</u>, p. 184.
39. <u>Landscape Gardening Studies</u>, p. 34.
40. <u>Landscape Gardening Studies</u>, p. 35
41. <u>How to Plan the Home Grounds</u>, p. 187.
42. <u>How to Plan the Home Grounds</u>, pp. 184-85
43. <u>How to Plan the Home Grounds</u>, p. 185.
44. Ibid.
45. <u>How to Plan the Home Grounds</u>, pp. 187-88.
46. Ibid.
47. <u>How to Plan the Home Grounds</u>, p. 165.
48. Ibid.
49. <u>Landscape Gardening Studies</u>, p. 24.
50. <u>How to Plan the Home Grounds</u>, pp. 166-67.
51. <u>The Art of Landscape Architecture</u>, p. 295.

The Border Row cottages along Hillside Walk - Hollyhock, Marigold, and Larkspur (from l to r) - as viewed from Rosebank.

Looking east up Cherokee Road, ca. 1910, at Cherokee cottage.

The Cottages

"One of Father's greatest pleasures was in building and furnishing houses, particularly working out plans with a friendly and artistic architect. Mr. Gilbert fulfilled these requirements; and I really believe Father had about as much pleasure from his building in Asheville as he did from anything in his life. I think every time he built a new cottage he felt like a little boy who buys a new toy—that he really should not put so much money into the venture, but it was so much fun!" (Thomas Wadley Raoul, The Family of Raoul)

From the start, the Raouls had planned for more than just another mountain resort hotel. To compete against the highly successful Battery Park, Kenilworth, and Swannanoa Hotels, and the numerous boarding houses in Asheville, they decided to develop their mountainside property in a special way, to respond to the "great want felt for houses and grounds of moderate dimension and expense."

By choosing Bradford Gilbert and Samuel Parsons as architect and landscape architect, the Raouls brought together two men who could apply the latest design concepts to the plan and make the most of the challenging mountain setting.

From their collaboration came the building of The Manor Inn, "a place as nearly like a home as a public house can well be" surrounded by picturesque cottages that, together, comprised one of this nation's earliest planned residential parks.

Planned Residential Communities

"When you look at the place now you are impressed with the fact that in a few years its whole appearance will be changed—it will be a grove of trees with houses around and among them." (Gaston Raoul to his mother from Albemarle Lodge, May 11, 1903)

As the United States became more urbanized, planners and designers began to look at new models of community planning. Albemarle Park, in the mountains of western North Carolina, was one of the first communities developed for such a difficult and steep site. It was probably influenced by several earlier planned communities that had received wide recognition as excellent examples of comprehensive planning.

Acknowledgement of the importance of

Milfoil cottage's front porch, with its heavy timbers and decorative shingling in the gable, 1991.

At the time the first cottage, Columbus, was built, in 1898, the area directly north of Albemarle Park was still farm land.

integrating new construction with the natural landscape had been growing since the 1850s.

One of the first planned communities during this period was Llewellyn Park, a residential suburban development in the foothills of the Orange Mountains of New Jersey, a collaboration of Llewellyn P. Haskell and architect Alexander Jackson Davis in 1852.

Though not on as difficult terrain as Albemarle Park, "the natural features of meadows, dells, woodlands, brooks, etc., were enhanced by the judicious placing of arbors, summer houses, gazebos, and rustic bridges, and the various parts were made accessible by winding drives sympathetic to the contours of the countryside. Residential lots were of irregular shape and sufficiently large to provide personal privacy. Dwellings were built in the quaint styles provided by the period." (Clay Lancaster, The American Bungalow, 1880-1930)

Unfortunately, only the gatehouse and one original cottage survive today, but the concept of incorporating the natural landscape in the overall plan was to be a foundation of future community design.

"The direct descendent of Llewellyn Park is Tuxedo Park, in the Catskill Mountains about thirty miles northwest of New York City." (Clay Lancaster, The American Bungalow, 1880-1930)

This community was originally developed by tobacco magnate Pierre Lorillard as a hunting reservation for himself and his friends.

Planned with the same sensitivity to the terrain as Llewellyn Park, this development became a rural retreat for much of New York's high society. The cottages and other structures in Tuxedo Park, many of them designed by architect Bruce Price in the mid-1880s, were not unlike those in Albemarle Park. The designs for the rustic clubhouse, gatehouse and forty cottages were widely published and may have served as models for Gilbert and the Raouls. The architecture of both Tuxedo Park and Albemarle Park includes some of the most imaginative and playful designs of the Shingle Style period.

Much of the special and enduring quality of Albemarle Park comes from the remarkable palette of residential designs chosen by the Raouls for their development and the integration of these structures into the mountain landscape.

Two developments in architecture had a profound effect on the planning of Albemarle Park's cottages—the growing maturation of the Shingle Style, a design trend that was enormously popular at the time, and the change in family living habits signified by the Bungalow movement.

The Shingle Style

"He [William Greene Raoul] was a master craftsman with the tools of a carpenter, and taught me to use them.

"He would lay my small hand by his, of which it was the replica, and say, 'William, when you see a man with hands like ours, short stubby fingers, the same size all the way up and down, that man can use his hands. That is the hand of an artisan.' " (William Greene Raoul, Jr., The Family of Raoul, quoting from his autobiography, The Rolling Stone)

William Greene Raoul, though professionally trained as an engineer, devoted much of his life to dabbling in his avocation of architecture. He was well read, a man who traveled extensively, and was knowledgeable about the latest developments of the architectural profession. For The Manor, the centerpiece of Albemarle Park, he chose the theme of "an English Inn in America." The architecture of the Shingle Style was well suited to expressing that concept both for the Inn and the cottages.

In the late 1870s and through the 1880s, architects and builders were actively working to develop a style that was more informal and less extravagant in plan, spatial arrangement and exterior design. The Shingle Style emerged from earlier periods of architectural design, the Colonial Revival and the Queen Anne styles, both of which had their roots in the less formal architecture of the English country manor houses of the late Middle Ages.

Clover cottage, ca. 1898, faces the porte cochere of The Manor Inn.

The Shingle Style, however, was a truly American design movement. It used building materials that were sympathetic with the landscape—common, low-cost, wood shingles which were readily available to the builder, stained in warm, natural tones and combined with trim detailing that was simpler than that used in preceding styles.

Most importantly, architects began to design homes for more open and informal lifestyles. Homes of the Queen Anne style were designed with both living halls and living rooms or parlors. The designs of Shingle Style homes were centered on "simplicity and informality in the shape of one large and open living area, both hall and living room." (Vincent J. Scully, The Shingle Style and The Stick Style)

This approach is evident in the first five cottages of Albemarle Park—Clover, Columbus, Clio, Clematis, and Cherokee. Each combines several sleeping rooms with one central common space, a large living room. Kitchens and dining rooms were not included in these

Galax cottage, an excellent example of the Dutch Revival Shingle Style, built in 1902 in just four months.

can architecture when the Raouls commissioned Bradford Gilbert to design The Manor Inn, the Lodge (Gatehouse), and the first five cottages. There was an extensive body of published work on the style by such important architects as McKim, Mead & White, Peabody & Stearns, Bruce Price, and others who had already produced many splendid residences.

In 1890, Gilbert designed the Raoul residence at 708 Peachtree in Atlanta, and it's obvious by this and other commissions that he had become quite adept at designing in the Shingle Style.

"Perhaps he [Tom] has not, in his description of The Manor project, sufficiently emphasized the fun which Father and Mr. Gilbert had in playing with all kinds of unconventional and charming buildings." (Mary Raoul Millis, The Family of Raoul)

With his work in Albemarle Park, Gilbert displays his excellent skills at combining the Shingle Style with Dutch Colonial Revival, Half-timbered Tudor, Rustic, and Chalet styles to create a pleasant, evocative European village atmosphere. This eclectic use of the Shingle Style was common in the Bungalow Movement, the other major architectural influence on Albemarle Park.

early cottages, as guests ate all of their meals at The Manor.

The focus of each Albemarle Park cottage living room is its fireplace. Though their designs vary, they are all primarily monumental in scale. Many have large, curved openings of rough stone or brick, and at least one incorporates an inglenook with built-in bench seats framing the hearth.

The remaining cottages built by the Raouls were "housekeeping cottages," complete with kitchens, pantries, and dining rooms. Many of these cottages also had an above-grade lower level, where quarters were provided for servants brought by the guests.

The Shingle Style was cresting in Ameri-

The Bungalow Movement

"The house is fine and pretty...The wild flowers are so beautiful here that there is no trouble to find as much decoration as our vases can hold...But the greatest charms of Albemarle are the coolness and the sweet birds. They are the first sounds in the morning (unless the laundress raises her voice in song) and they sing all day long. It certainly seems strange to be in Asheville this way with the woods just outside the front door." **(Agnes Raoul to her mother from Milfoil Cottage, June 11, 1899)**

Sometime in the 1880s, the strides made by architects in the development of the Shingle Style began to evolve into what has been recognized as the Bungalow Movement. Originally, the Shingle Style was used primarily for summer "cottages" for the wealthy of the northeast, or for large seaside inns. Soon, however, architects and builders began to adapt it for use in the designs of smaller homes and bungalows for families of more modest means.

"Bungalows have been built in the Western Stick style, the Prairie style, the Mission style, and a host of Colonial styles from Spanish to English to Dutch. Frequently, bungalows borrowed detail and form from the Swiss chalet, the Japanese temple, the Chinese pagoda, or the log cabin of the frontiersman." (Tony P. Wrenn, AIA from his Introduction to <u>Bungalows, Camps and Mountain Houses</u>)

What makes Albemarle Park so important,

The main sitting room in Galax today, light and airy, with its rough brick fireplace and wrap-around staircase.

architecturally, is its broad sampling of the many varied styles of the Bungalow Movement and the successful integration of each cottage with its neighbors in the landscape.

In 1891, R.A. Briggs, in his book <u>Bungalows and Country Residences,</u> described a bungalow "as a little country house—a homey, cosy little place, with verandah and balconies and the plan so arranged as to ensure complete comfort, with a feeling of rusticity and ease."

The Rauols and their guests in Albemarle Park were seeking exactly that, in comfortable, well-designed cottages, nestled in the woods away from their busy urban lives in places like Atlanta, Savannah, and New York.

Clematis Cottage, an example of the half-timbered Tudor style with heavy pebble-dash stucco, ca. 1903, viewed from the curved drive beside Cherokee cottage.

ed with its setting. Considered as a period, the title bungalow can be given to all detached residential buildings produced during the first quarter of the twentieth century, and to others related to them that belong in the two decades before and almost a decade after that twenty-five year interval. As a movement the building of bungalows was governed by principles such as simplicity, vitality, and straightforwardness, and these applied to every aspect of the phenomenon: its exterior and its affinity to the environment, the relation between outside and inside, its interior and how it best could serve the purpose of sheltering and providing a pleasant atmosphere for the modern family." (Clay Lancaster, <u>The American Bungalow, 1880-1930</u>)

The cottages of Albemarle Park were sensitively oriented on the hillside, to take advantage of the mountain views and the summer sun, yet also achieve a measure of privacy while maintaining a sense of community intimacy.

"The bungalow ideal of environmental submersion made for a neighborhood unity, which is infinitely more pleasing than the staccato effect of suburban developments today." (Clay Lancaster, <u>The American Bungalow, 1880-1930</u>)

In many cases the landscape not only surrounded a cottage but began to engulf it, as vines and creepers climbed chimneys and walls. From the start, the Raouls named the cottages for plants that were indigenous to the Appalachian mountain region: Kalmia, Galax, Laurel, Hollyhock, Clematis, Laurel,

The Bungalow Movement thrived in Asheville, with its good, year-round climate of moderate winters and temperate summers. The Shingle Style was adapted by architects and builders to integrate both the indoor and outdoor living spaces into one.

"The Bungalow in the United States was a type of house, a period of architecture, and a movement. In terms of the first category it can be recognized by its form, which is low, overshadowed by the roof, restrained in the manner of style, subdued in color, and blend-

Pine Tree, Clover, etc.

The ones they didn't give plant names, like Columbus Cottage, which was the first one to be built, had names of special significance to the family.

"I remember when Father and I were staking out Columbus Cottage, and he was wondering if he could afford to build it, the mail was brought to him, and in it was a check for $1,400.00, a dividend from the Columbus (Ga.) Iron Works, just about the estimated cost of the cottage. Hence the name." (Thomas Wadley Raoul, The Family of Raoul)

Snug Harbor cottage, built later, probably derives its name from Sailor's Snug Harbor, the Seamen's retirement home on Staten Island near where they lived when they were in New York.

Cottage Design and Construction

"...Albemarle is looking very beautiful...I still feel as if I knew every brick and plank in it." (Thomas Wadley Raoul to his Mother from The Manor, May 2, 1908)

Most of the cottages in Albemarle Park were built with great speed. Even such large cottages as Galax were built in less than four months. Thomas Wadley Raoul managed the construction of each one, though he noted, "of course Father kept a close eye on the operations." William Greene Raoul reviewed all the designs prepared by Gilbert and, no doubt, had

a hand in the design of all of the early cottages.

In a letter to their mother dated January 18, 1910, Thomas and his younger brother Loring included sketches for Kalmia cottage's facade design which, according to Tom, their father was designing.

Thomas also sent his parents sketches of his ideas for Manzanita cottage in January, 1906, while he was recuperating in Oracle, Arizona from one of many bouts of tuberculosis.

Work on the cottages and landscape of Albemarle Park became a family enterprise.

Gaston, Loring and Norman helped with the surveying and road construction. The Raoul daughters, Agnes, Rebecca and Rosine, enjoyed getting involved in the finishing details, deciding on some of the interior colors.

William Greene Raoul and his wife Mary "would spend hours wandering around together and deciding on a tree here, or a plantation of shrubs there, or a bed of flowers around The Manor or cottages." (Mary Raoul Millis, The Family of Raoul)

They were a family in love not only with the design of Albemarle Park but also with all of the details of its construction.

At this time, Gustav Stickley, through his magazine, The Craftsman, and the production, promotion and distribution of his furniture and interior furnishings, was gaining adherents to his theories on living and design.

Stickley was one of the leading proponents of the Arts and Crafts Movement at the turn of the century, which embraced many fields of design besides architecture—furniture, textiles, pottery, jewelry, and

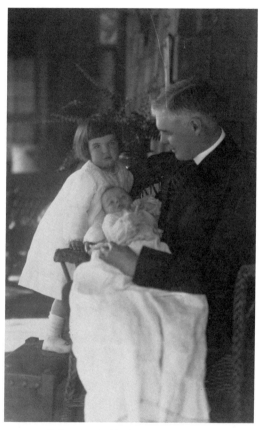

Thomas Wadley Raoul with his two daughters, Kathleen and newly born Jane, on the porch of Manzanita cottage in 1915.

gardening—and called for the harmonious integration of all design elements.

Stickley published hundreds of house designs in various bungalow styles, and wrote extensively on how houses should harmonize with their surroundings in materials, color, siting, and landscape.

It's highly likely that the Raouls had

Manzanita Cottage

Manzanita cottage, a rustic Shingle Style cottage built in 1906 as Thomas Wadley Raoul's "bachelor cottage" in the woods. After he married in 1910, Thomas added a master bedroom wing at the right corner.

Manzanita's living room, with its rough plastered walls and ceilings, heart pine flooring and brick fireplace.

Four different doors lead out onto Manzanita's deep, high-ceilinged porch which looks out on to The Circle.

become familiar with Stickley's ideas. From letters and photographs of interiors that still exist, we know that the Raouls furnished the cottages in the style Stickley was advocating and producing for a "comfortable" Craftsman home. Mission oak, wicker and rustic twig furniture was ordered from New York and Grand Rapids, Michigan to furnish the Inn and cottages.

In How to Build a Bungalow Stickley wrote, "the exterior presents a combination of materials easily obtainable in any locality, which may be put together by any man hav-ing the slightest knowledge of mason-work and carpentry. The building is constructed in the usual manner of balloon framed houses, covered with sheathing and tarred paper, over which are placed large pine, cedar, or red-wood shingles, as are most available in the locality in which the building is situated. It is purposed to stain these shingles a dull burnt sienna color, and the roof in a color technically known as silver-stain. This sien-na color, in a very short time, comes to look like an autumn oak leaf; and this, together with the rough stone of the large chimney, tends to tie the building to its surroundings and to give it the seeming of a growth rather than a creation. The large and spacious veranda, [and] the simple forms of the roof...tend to give the construction an air of genuine homeliness: a quality in design much sought for and not always attained."

Applying these principles to the design of their cottages, the Raouls built with a rich palette of materials.

The siding they used consisted of evenly coursed rows of split oak, cedar or chestnut shingles. They used the same material for the roof. The stone that was used for the massive chimneys was quarried right on the site by the Raouls. They also made use of this resource for landscaping, crushing the rock to use as a base for the macadam roads, and using groupings of large rocks as landscape features along the curves of the roads and drives, to keep horses and carriages from straying on the lawns.

For the more rustic cottages, whole tree trunks were incorporated into the structure of the houses, both as exterior and interior features.

The use of porches, balconies, and enclosed sleeping porches is one of the most important design features of the Bungalow Movement that one finds in almost all of the Albemarle Park cottages. The living room, made less formal in Shingle Style design, came to incorporate both interior and exterior spaces with the advent of the Bungalow Movement. Porches and terraces adjoined living rooms and bedrooms, allowing family life to flow to the outside in good weather. In a climate like Asheville's, this element of architectural design was essential to a well-designed and healthful residence.

The highly decorative "painted lady" color schemes for houses of earlier eras was forsaken for a new approach. "Colors were almost always muted and organic. The bunga-low was not a stark white or yellow house on a hill, nor was the interior as grim or dark as its Victorian counterpart. Interior colors were light and airy. Colors that could absorb '50 to 85 per cent of the light' such as scarlet,

Crow's Nest cottage, built in 1905, was Thomas Wadley Raoul's "honeymoon cottage" briefly, after he married Helen Doyle Bennett in 1910.

crimsons, browns, and deep buffs, were shunned, for light was of supreme importance in the bungalow." (Tony P. Wrenn, AIA in his Introduction to <u>Bungalows, Camps and Mountain Houses</u>)

To this end, the cottages were designed with an abundance of windows and doors, to fill the interiors with light and strengthen the connection of the indoors to the outdoors.

This also allowed the guests to take advantage of the mountain breezes and the

cool night air that made Asheville so attrac-tive as a summer enclave.

Cottages in the Rustic Style

"Should my health improve and it looks as if I can again live in Asheville part of each year we will build a little house for me up in the woods near Galax. Father objected to this very strenuously at first but since I have not been so well the poor

The porch(left) outside Crow's Nest's two-story living room (right) looks out over the open greensward beside Cherokee Road, where archery contests and croquet tournaments were held for guests during the hey-day of The Manor Inn.

man wants to do anything in the world for me. I think I will be very much better located in my own quarters both for health and comfort. My idea is for a simple cottage to cost $1,000 or possibly $1,500. My idea is to make this to my wants but to make it so that when I cease to use it it can be converted into a modest housekeeping cottage by enclosing the North porch for a kitchen and changing the sitting room to a dining room. I think this quite an original and satisfactory plan but I consider it all a castle in the air until I get a little farther along with the 'cure.' " **(Thomas Wadley Raoul to his sister, Mary, from Oracle, Arizona, January 15, 1906)**

Manzanita was Tom's own home, his "bachelor" cottage. He and his father designed and built it in 1906 as a place in the woods where he could recuperate.

After he married Helen Doyle Bennett in 1910, he set to making improvements and additions to the cottage to accommodate their lives and allow them ample space for the later addition of their two children, Kathleen and Jane.

"Everything in Manzanita seems to be working out so well and it is so much more liveable and lived in looking than I thought it would ever be." (Thomas Wadley Raoul to his mother from Manzanita Cottage, August, 13, 1910)

Possum Trot cottage, built by 1913 in the Rustic Shingle Style, incorporated elements of traditional Appalachian architecture.

applied texture that complements the rustic exterior.

Other rustic cottages like Possum Trot and Dogwood harken back more to the vernacular architecture of the Appalachian mountains.

Dogwood was built as a home for William Greene and Mary Raoul in 1910. It sits on a commanding mountainside site and has panoramic views of Mt. Pisgah and the western range from its large log porch. Its chimneys were originally wrapped in logs all the way to the peak, giving it somewhat of an appearance of a traditional mountain cabin. Its pergolas of rough logs allowed for the vines to climb and enclose the porches, a feature that landscape architect Samuel Parsons so loved.

Another of the rustic cottages, and one of the most romantic, is Crow's Nest (ca. 1905), nestled in the woods near the Border Row cottages. Thomas called it "a dear" and thought it turned out much better than they had planned. A visitor to Crow's Nest enters the small front doorway and is surprised by an impressive two story living room. The Arts and Crafts balustrade leads up to the small second floor bedroom where interior casement windows open onto the room below. One imagines this a home for an Appalachian Romeo and Juliet.

The plaster walls of this cottage feature an unusual, deeply incised grid pattern. It's as if the builder so liked the look of the unfinished plaster, scratched to accept the final coat, that he decided not to finish it. The living room and the lower level dining room both open onto large log porches that over-

With tree trunks supporting the roof over its enormous L-shaped porch, and the three chimneys of massive, rough, gray granite with deep set mortar joints, it epitomizes the rustic style cottages.

Manzanita is named for a western evergreen shrub or groundcover of the barberry family and is the only one of the rustic cottages to have a distinct Japanese influence.

The large central hip roof with 4'-0" deep overhangs and flared rafter ends give the cottage the flavor of an oriental pagoda. Thomas may have grown fond of oriental design during his trips to Los Angeles and up the west coast, or from reports of Japan and the Phillipines he received from his Mother and older sister, Mary.

The plaster inside has a rough, hand

Dogwood cottage was built in 1910 as William Greene Raoul's own summer home, looking out over The Circle from its hillside perch on Canterbury Road.

The living room in Dogwood is centered around its large brick fireplace and inglenook.

look the central greensward that lies along Cherokee Road.

Two of the later cottages, Wildfell and Brown Bear (c.1913-14), also incorporate some rustic detailing in their exterior design, though they were originally clad in lapped siding. Their large porches are built of log structural supports and simple log railings, stripped of bark and left natural to age to a dark warm chestnut brown.

By the time these cottages were built, William Greene Raoul had died and it was Thomas' choice to build in the rustic style he obviously preferred. He wrote to his Mother in June of 1913, "I have a surveyor at work on the park and hope he will finish his labors in two weeks when we will begin to plat the place off anew. I have not yet begun to cut the trees as I have a plan to populate all the upper part of the park with 'Adirondak Camps' for summer use only. I believe if we can show the summer visitor how he can get a comfortable summer camp from $2,000 to $3,000 he will be willing to own his own summer home."

Cottages in the Half-Timbered Tudor Style

Half-timbered tudor cottages are characterized by a division of the use of materials between the foundation, first and second floors. The base of these cottages are typically constructed of the gray granite that the Raouls quarried on site.

The exterior finish of the first floor is a heavy pebble-dash stucco. This "pebble-dashing" used stone aggregate applied with standard stucco to give a roughly textured finish that was then painted, usually a light color.

The stucco is often sectioned into separate areas by heavy, pegged timbering at corners, around windows and between the first and second floor levels. The second floor is usually shingled and projects beyond the first with a splayed skirt of shingles or a bracketed cantilever, and has windows with shingled eyebrows that project above them.

Another detail of this style was the use of

Clio cottage, built in 1900, was the only example of the Chalet Style in Albemarle Park, and had four guest rooms on each floor around a central stairwell.

A Cottage in the Swiss Chalet Style

Clio cottage (ca. 1902) is the only Albemarle Park cottage inspired by the architecture of the European Swiss Chalet, a style typical of the high mountains of the Alps. Though European in its roots, it was an architectural style that was easily adapted to this steep hillside site. Although its footprint is a simple rectangle, Clio is characterized by open porches, suspended balconies entered from the second floor bedrooms through french doors, and enormous wood brackets supporting the deep overhanging roof.

Designed by Bradford Gilbert, the building is ornamented with a large gable-end wooden screen suspended between the heavy timber bracketing that has cutouts in the shapes of diamonds, circles, and ellipses, and a wood medallion at the peak of the roof. What was emblazoned on this medallion and why this cottage was the only one built in this style has been lost over time.

Cottages in the Dutch Colonial Revival Style

Galax (c.1902) and Rosebank (c.1905) are two, very large, shingled cottages designed in the Dutch Colonial Revival Style. Both sit on the sides of steep banks and, though appearing to have only two stories on the entry side, each possesses a full three-to-four story facade on the downhill side.

Judging from William Greene Raoul's

heavy timber brackets to support window bays and eaves.

One of the finest examples of this style is Clover cottage. Clover and Columbus were the first two cottages built, and were finished in 1898, prior to The Manor's completion.

Clover sits at the corner of Cherokee and Terrace Roads and was passed by every guest that entered The Manor's porte cochere.

Bradford Gilbert designed this cottage with a tapered stone chimney that stands sentinel over the road, and with a large turret and wraparound open porch that projects out over the intersection. The entrance facade is composed of two splayed gables on either side of a truncated turret and another porch facing the Inn.

Clematis cottage (ca. 1901), another of the first five cottages associated with The Manor, is also built in this half-timbered style. In this cottage, the second floor roof sweeps down to the first floor level where it becomes the roof of several deep porches.

notes on Samuel Parsons' site plan, the Raouls had been contemplating expanding the southern boundary of Albemarle Park as early as 1899. When they decided to go ahead with the construction of Rosebank cottage, they finally purchased the additional land along Charlotte Street that they had been eyeing. There was a large amount of excavation required for the foundation of Rosebank and this new property was a good place to dump the dirt. It later became the site for several more cottages and the Public Garage for The Manor's guests.

For Rosebank and Galax, wood shingles were used for both the siding and the roof material. The windows have diamond-paned upper sashes, popular in cottage design, and, especially at Rosebank, they are quite playfully arranged. Windows of various sizes and shapes are tied together with simple trim.

The variety works well, and the overall design is unified by the large gambrel roofs and a wrap-around porch. The use of the gambrel roofs, slightly cantilevered over the first floor level, is characteristic of the Dutch Revival style. Family correspondence documents that William Greene Raoul worked with a young man named Harry Tyler to design Galax cottage and the Clubhouse. Tyler, presumably an architect, was an Atlanta gentleman and friend of his daughter, Rebecca Raoul.

Twin Oaks, ca. 1920, shows the influence of a different designer on the later structures of Albemarle Park. It was the only cottage built as an apartment building.

Cottages with Queen Anne Style Influences

Though the Queen Anne style had reached the end of its popularity in the Northeast by the mid-1880s, two of the early Manor cottages, though predominantly in the shingle style, retain certain exterior elements that were popular in that movement.

Shamrock cottage (c.1898) has a very large, three-story, gable-roofed bay in which a grouping of three windows is set at each floor, giving it a verticality that is uncharacteristic of the other cottages. It combines elements of the half-timbered Tudor style through its use of shingling and pebble-dash,

Dahlia cottage, built in 1906 along with its mirror-imaged neighbor, Daffodil, was one of the Border Row Cottages, along the southern edge of Albemarle Park, on Orchard Place.

Marigold cottage, built in 1907 along Hillside Walk, was identical to Hollyhock, its uphill neighbor.

Larkspur cottage was on the new property the Raouls bought when they decided to build Rosebank. It was moved and made one of the five Border Row cottages.

but it features a large gable end with a feather pattern of heavy timbers, far more decorative than the shingled gable ends of the other early cottages. While the design of the cottage does incorporate deep porches tucked under the roof of the house, more traditional of bungalow design than the Queen Anne style, it seems to have been a hybrid of elements and maybe a transitional design on the way to the more picturesque Albemarle Park cottages.

Orchard cottage (c.1899) shares some similarities with Shamrock, with two pairs of three narrow windows stacked above each other in a gable-ended bay, but it is balanced by another adjacent gabled bay above the front entry door. This cottage, with its wrap-around porch, simple undecorated railing pickets, brick foundation and wood shingling is closer to the pure Shingle Style architecture. The Queen Anne influence gives both these cottages a more formal and urban feeling than later cottages.

The Border Row Cottages

"Father was always enthusiastic about Asheville...and he often stopped over between New York, Atlanta, and Mexico...On one of his trips when he was considering some expenditure, he said that he would not give his answer then, but would write me from New York. He said that Asheville air affected him like champagne; it went to his head; and he was apt to do things for which he would be sorry in the grim dawn of New York. But building was in Father's blood, and from time to time he would sneak in another cottage." (Thomas Wadley Raoul, <u>The Family of Raoul</u>)

It seems it was William Greene Raoul's enthusiasm for building rather than his concern for profits that spurred Albemarle Park's continued development.

At the extreme southern edge of Albemarle Park, Thomas Wadley Raoul built five small and less pretentious housekeeping cot-

Orchard cottage, built in 1899, was one of two early cottages with Queen Anne Style details.

Shamrock, built in 1898 while The Manor was under construction, also contains many Queen Anne Syle influences in its design.

Snug Harbor, ca. 1917, faces Charlotte Street and was most likely named after Sailors' Snug Harbor, a seamen's retirement community on Staten Island, New York near which the Raoul family lived during the 1890s.

tages. By 1903, Thomas notes, "We seem to be able to do a land office business in the housekeeping cottages, and Father wants to go ahead at a rapid rate with them."

What may have spurred on this development of the Border Row cottages was the existence of a small cottage adjacent to Rosebank.

Thomas wrote to his sister, Mary, in January, 1906, "Do you remember the little 2x4 house right near Rosebank which we did not own? Well we bought it and quite a large lot before I left and we expect to roll it to the back line next summer and build two houses of the same class (if I can hold Father down)."

Daffodil (ca.1906) and Dahlia (ca.1906), both built in the Shingle Style, are mirror-image copies of each other. Inside, the central staircase, with simple Craftsman style detailing, takes you to the several upstairs bedrooms tucked under the roof gables, including one that is playfully located on a mid-landing up a small separate set of stairs.

Marigold (ca.1907) and Hollyhock (ca.1907), built in the Tudoresque style with shingles and pebble-dash, are exact copies of each other. Together with the cottage that was bought and moved, Larkspur, they are the Border Row cottages, with front entrances off Hillside Walk, the only sidewalk "street" address in Asheville. Though the Border Row cottages are sited close together all along a line, the drop in grade down to Charlotte Street and a buffer of planting between the them affords the tenants a measure of privacy that is rarely achieved on such small lots.

Other Cottages

There are several cottages which, though considered primary structures that contribute to Albemarle Park's unique historic character, were built by individuals other than the Raouls and are somewhat different in character than those that were built as part of the original Albemarle Park development.

Breezemont (ca. 1914) is the most prominent of the cottages that were built by private individuals in Albemarle Park.

It overlooks all of the other cottages and the Manor from its setting just below the large stone wall that marks the east entrance to Albemarle Park from Sunset Drive.

Herbert Miles, prominent in Asheville at the time, commissioned the architect Richard Sharp Smith to design a home for his family to be built on the lot he bought from The Albemarle Park Company in 1913. Smith had been the representative of architect Richard Morris Hunt during the construction of Biltmore Estate for the Vanderbilts and saw in Asheville a burgeoning construction market in which he could ply his design trade.

Though this was Smith's only Albemarle Park commission, his architectural legacy lives on in other neighborhoods, including Montford and Chestnut Hill, as well as in downtown Asheville.

Breezemont Cottage has been described as Colonial Revival or somewhat Georgian in design, with its large central gable, its palladian window and the dentil trim on the exterior, but it is purely Craftsman in design on the interior. The windows are wood casements accompanied by fixed transoms and simple oak trim.

This is one of the few cottages that does not have many porches but, instead, relies more on open terraces adjacent to family rooms.

Chipmunk (ca. 1922), Chestnut Hill (ca. 1922), and Twin Oaks (ca.1922) were all later additions to Albemarle Park, and, though the architect of these is not known,

Breezemont, located high above the other cottages in Albemarle Park, was designed by Richard Sharp Smith for Herbert Miles on land Miles had bought from The Albemarle Park Company in 1914.

they are all quite similar in style. Chestnut Hill and Chipmunk sit side by side on the south facing bank above The Circle. Both are Tudoresque, covered with a smooth stucco with half-timbering and brick quoining at the corners. Chipmunk uses intersecting gambrel roofs with dormers to give it a more picturesque quality than either Chestnut Hill or Twin Oaks. Twin Oaks was the only cottage built specifically as an apartment building with individual living rooms. It does mimic its neighbor, Cherokee Cottage by incorporating two story porches on either side of the building. It, too, was built with

The interior of Breezemont belies the formal exterior. The living room shown in these two views displays an extensive use of Arts & Crafts detailing.

smooth stucco and brick quoining, but, like Chipmunk, it sits on a foundation of rough stone, quite characteristic of earlier cottages.

Pine Tree, Alva Glen, Raven's Nest, Locust, The Willows, Fir Tree, and Snug Harbor are contributing structures built before 1925. The lots on which they sit were platted—and the cottages sometimes named—as part of the original development, but they weren't built by the Raouls. The lots were pur-

chased by individuals from either the Raouls after the death of William Greene Raoul or, after 1920, from E.W. Grove or his estate. Most of these structures have taken their design styles from the original Albemarle Park cottages and contribute to the overall integrity of the planned residential community. A sprinkling of post-World War II structures were built on the few remaining lots, with more or less the same successful integration.

The remarkable intimacy and character of Albemarle Park was decisively shaped by the creative use of design variations for the cottages and the special way they all nestle in the woods and cling to the hillsides. Their common palette of materials, the manner in which each was sited in relation to its neighbors, and the extra thought that was given to the overall planting of the grounds—these all contribute to creating a unified character in Albemarle Park.

The Manor ballroom was the site of many elegant and festive affairs, such as this fancy dress ball given by Mrs. John Kerr Connally in 1914.

Jane (left) and Kathleen Raoul dressed for a children's performance of "Lil Bo Peep" given at The Manor.

The Social Life of Albemarle Park

"The fancy dress ball at Albemarle Manor last evening in celebration of St. Valentine's day was the pronounced social success anticipated." (The Asheville Citizen, Feb. 15, 1899)

The social life for the guests in Albemarle Park, and for many Ashevillians, centered around the Manor Inn. From its earliest days of operation, cultural events of all kinds were planned for the benefit of guests and the community. The Raoul family, athletic, well-read and well-travelled, and deeply involved in the cultural and educational life of Atlanta, were intent on incorporating a variety of recreational and educational opportunities into the life of Albemarle Park, their mountain home.

Their sponsorship of events was motivated by personal generosity and interest as well as by purely business reasons. During its first month of operation, Thomas Wadley Raoul sponsored the first of many charity events held at the Manor. This was to assist The Flower Mission, an organization formed to benefit the local hospital.

Billed as a musical entertainment, it also included a tour of The Manor. As Thomas stated in a letter to his mother, "I think the latter attraction proved greater than the first.

Everyone was charmed with the house and I think it was the very best thing we could have done to advertise the house." He was correct in that perception as The Manor came to serve as one of Asheville's centers of community life in the years that followed.

Balls, dances, musical performances, and plays were just some of the events held at The Manor. Some of these, especially the balls, found the Inn, and often its guests, transformed, as described in this report of an 1899 St. Valentine's Ball from The Asheville Citizen. "The rooms were lavishly and artistically decorated with evergreens, in the deep shades of which had been suggestively arranged blood red hearts arrow-pierced and bleeding. In the decoration of the ball pendant were the words 'Hearts are trumps,' traced in brilliant letters."

Guests came dressed as such characters as, "the Queen of Hearts, Narcissus, a Colonial Dame, Mephistopheles, a Court Gentleman, and a Greek slave."

As business at The Manor increased, the importance of its cultural life was reinforced with the addition of a ballroom in the 1903 wing. Plays for adults and children provided a constant source of family entertainment. Photos and letters document a variety of perfor-

Shakespeare in the Park, in The Circle. The author Thomas Wolfe is reputed to have acted in these outdoor performances.

The lawn beside the Clubhouse and the tennis courts was used quite often for children's performances. A reenactment of <u>Alice in Wonderland</u>, with Thomas Wadley Raoul's daughters, is underway here, ca. 1919.

mances from small locally-written amateur plays to children's reenactments of Alice in Wonderland.

Music was also important and The Manor sponsored weekly evening musical concerts. "We have a fine orchestra and they play on the stone terrace under the light while the audience sit around the porches and listen." (Thomas Wadley Raoul)

Since life in Albemarle Park centered on its beautiful mountain setting, many of these same events took advantage of the temperate climate and were performed outside in the public greenspaces. Pianos and persian carpets were brought out onto the lawns, as elegantly dressed guests sat in the cool shade of the oaks.

The gently sloped, grassy bowl at the center of The Circle became a natural amphitheater for such events as Shakespearian plays in which at least one illustrious local actor, the writer Thomas Wolfe, performed.

In 1902, Thomas embarked on a major construction project to broaden the opportunities for social entertainment and increase the revenue of his business venture. He built a Clubhouse, "The Albemarle Club," which he also called The Casino, adjacent to the tennis court near the Lodge. Not unlike other resort developments around the country, this was to be a recreational center for guests of the Inn. "The Albemarle Club with its bowling alley, tennis courts and pool and billiard tables, provides a place of amusement within the Park, and frequent tournaments are held there." (from an early Manor brochure)

A piano and Persian carpet grace the lawn of the Clubhouse for a performance of <u>Alice in Wonderland</u> under the trees along Cherokee Road.

This proved to be a profitable addition. Together with The Manor, it allowed the Raouls to expand their ability to host various conventions that came to Asheville, with "smokers" at the Clubhouse and fine luncheons at the Inn for such groups as the American Institute of Electrical Engineers and the Mississippi Valley Medical Association.

Outdoor recreation was extremely important. For the Raouls, a pleasant summer vacation wouldn't be complete without a wide array of recreational and athletic activities.

Though plagued by tuberculosis, Thomas Wadley Raoul had been the captain of the Georgia Tech football team during his college years, and was an accomplished horseman who helped organize yearly horse shows in Asheville.

The stable of Albemarle Park, one of the few original buildings that have been lost through the years, housed not only his personal horses, but horses that were available for the guests.

Albemarle Park was located at the north-

Club House, The Manor.   ASHEVILLE, N. C.

The Clubhouse (top), also called The Casino in the early years, was built in 1902 next to the tennis courts, and included a billiards room for the men and a bowling alley for the women. The billiards room (bottom), with the bowling alley visible through the doorway at the rear.

ern edge of Asheville, "...the ragged end of nowhere," according to Thomas Wadley Raoul in The Family of Raoul, when it was first built. Beyond it, just a short horse ride away, lay the mountains, offering panoramic views across the French Broad River valley to the high peaks of the Blue Ridge. Thomas advertised this feature in his promotional booklets. "The panorama of the distant mountains is so wonderful that it would justify a journey of miles to enjoy. Riding and driving are in high favor, and excellent harness and saddle horses may be secured at reasonable rates from The Manor liverymen. Splendid macadam roads lead out from Asheville for eight or ten miles in all directions, while the many woodland ways cannot be exhausted in weeks of riding and driving."

The young unmarried adults especially enjoyed social events such as "paper chases" and carriage rides for afternoon picnics. Driven by staff dressed in fine livery attire, carriages from The Manor were made available to any guests wanting to travel to the central train station or to other Asheville locations.

The entire Albemarle Park landscape was designed for recreation and relaxation. Guests could take quiet strolls among the cottages on the narrow footpaths and service drives, or wander up Cherokee Road into the mountains beyond Possum Trot and Breezemont cottages.

They could walk down to the broad grassy area below Crow's Nest and Orchard cottages to watch the croquet tournaments or compete in the archery contests held there.

Both the physical beauty and the healthful benefit of the outdoors was promoted in Manor brochures and advertisements. Here, Rebecca Raoul (center) and two friends are hiking in the mountains near The Manor.

Left: A children's performance in the ballroom, ca. 1919.

The children—"there were always twenty to thirty children" according to Albert Malone—were always kept busy, putting on pageants for their parents, on the lawn near the tennis court or in the large ballroom near the sweeping front lawn, or, in later years, playing on gym equipment that was erected near the Clubhouse.

When Thomas first came to Asheville to build The Manor he joined the Asheville Country Club, located at the end of Charlotte Street, a quarter mile away. In the beginning, he merely wanted to broaden his friendships with other residents in Asheville and offset his solitary bachelor's life.

Later, as his plans for Albemarle Park evolved, he developed a working arrangement with the Club that allowed him to advertise the golf links as an extra amenity for his guests, available for their use and enjoyment.

In 1905 he even tried to convince his Father to buy the golf links. He feared that the Club would lose it, and, if he and his father didn't take action, he would lose access to it for his guests. His Father wasn't interested at the time and the purchase was never made. Ironically, that course now serves the guests of the Grove Park Inn, Asheville's current premier resort inn, which played a major role in the slow decline of the Manor during the late 1920s and 1930s.

Guests were also encouraged to take advantage of the recreational and outdoor activities available across the mountain region. Thomas advertised, "Good quail

Loring Raoul with his horse outside of the stable behind The Manor, ca. 1909.

New Orleans Times/Picayune newspaper, would come up to Foxhall, the cottage he had built on a lot he had bought in the Park in 1914. He would delight the children as he sat in his olive green Lincoln, in a seersucker suit and panama hat, being driven around by his driver, Andrew.

Mrs. Farthing, from Lamar, Texas, was another regular guest. Her brother ran the Reconstruction Finance Corporation, appointed by President Franklin D. Roosevelt.

Even Al Jolson came to stay, quietly residing in Twin Oaks while he recovered from throat surgery.

According to Albert Malone, who was the son of long-term innkeeper, A. H. Malone, and was born and raised in Albemarle Park, the guests congregated each evening in the sitting room off the lobby entrance. Each Sunday and Monday evening, Clyde Spencer and his wife, with their string quartet, would play pleasant classical music. On the other nights there would be dances, with the big Steinway grand squeezed into the corner and all the furniture pushed to the walls.

Meanwhile, some guests played slot machines, or listened to the old Atwater-Kent radio in one or the other of the two rooms just off to the side.

When Christmas came, Mrs. Malone would put up a huge tree that filled the entire doorway at one side of the sitting room and gather beneath it a small mountain of brightly wrapped gifts for the staff and the guests.

The Manor and Albemarle Park flourished for more than thirty years, attracting

shooting may be found all around Asheville in season, and guides who know the country and can secure the required permits can be hired at small expense, together with well trained dogs. There is also good trout fishing within a radius of forty or fifty miles, and some near at hand on preserved lands."

During the 1920s and early 1930s, Albemarle Park flourished with guests who had made their name as pioneers in business and the arts, coming from all over the country.

Ken Smith, who made his fortune by selling Pepsodent Tooth Company to Lever Brothers, would arrive in his 1932 red Dusenberg roadster.

E. A. Fordtran, who was the owner of the

prominent guests from across the country. In every way, the activities that took place in Albemarle Park were meant to enrich the mind, body and spirit of those who found refuge there. But, as is the case with all things, times changed. New resorts opened and the social whirl moved away. The Manor slowly lost its luster and the guests moved on, to the new resort hotel nearby, the Grove Park Inn.

Kathleen Raoul in a carriage at the corner of The Circle and Terrace Road, ca. 1915.

Thomas Wadley Raoul, later in life.

The Later Years

"I suspect that it was she (Mother) who promoted the purchase of the Deaver farm in the beginning. From that time until the sad day in 1913, when Father died, Mother was just as much a part of the Asheville venture as he was. Mother never begrudged the money she saw going into it, and she always knew we would get it back.

"When he came to his investment in Albemarle Park which stood at around $250,000, he said that he never expected his heirs to get this back, and we would have just to do the best we could with it.

"After 1913 there was no one who had the time, the interest, or the means, to go on playing with Albemarle Park. The family decided that it should be put on a profitable basis. Looking towards that end, it was agreed that an addition to the main building should be built, and that some of the unproductive land and outlying cottages should be sold. This addition was made in 1913-1914, and cost far more than the original building. The addition was made, not with the idea of selling the property, but only to make it a more profitable enterprise.

"Just at this time, Mr. E. W. Grove, of St. Louis, was building "Grove Park Inn," and was spending money like water. The idea of selling our entire property to him occurred to Tom, and some advances were made, but Mr. Grove was not interested at that time.

"From 1914 to 1920 the enlarged Manor operated with great success, and Tom thought it would be a good time to again seek a customer. Not knowing that Mr. Grove had become interested, he offered it to another prospect. Mr. Grove must have learned what was going on, as an agent approached Tom with the idea that the property could now be sold to Mr. Grove. The result was highly gratifying, as the sale was made for over twice what we were willing to sell for in 1913.

"In 1920, seven years after Father's death, we sold the stock of the Albemarle Park Company to Mr. E. W. Grove, after having sold several of the cottages to outsiders. The entire sales netted well over a half million dollars." (Mary Raoul Millis, The Family of Raoul)

Thomas Wadley Raoul

"As a man and a citizen, Mr. Raoul was an aristocrat in aiming at the highest and best; he was a democrat spelled with a little 'd' in his association with others. He possessed fine talents as an organizer and manager, but he had no impulses leading him into efforts to impose his opinions upon others.

"In the town of that day reaching out toward city stature, Mr. Raoul soon became known for his fruitful ideas, his public spirit, and his clear and strong yet never aggressive convictions. In short, it seemed to many of that day that in Mr. Raoul there was another native son, with extraordinary abilities and idealism as a planner and builder.

"Like a sturdy oak of the Biltmore Forest: there was something like this in the fibre and quality of Thomas Wadley Raoul. He was never tossed about by varying winds of opinion and doctrine. In his views of political and social programs, and party creeds, he was a fine blend of the conservative liberal. He was in all things a devoted adopted son of Asheville and North Carolina." (Thomas Wadley Raoul's obituary in <u>The Asheville Citizen</u>)

This layout of Albemarle Park, from a promotional brochure, ca. 1910, represents the property the Raouls attempted to sell to E. W. Grove in 1913.

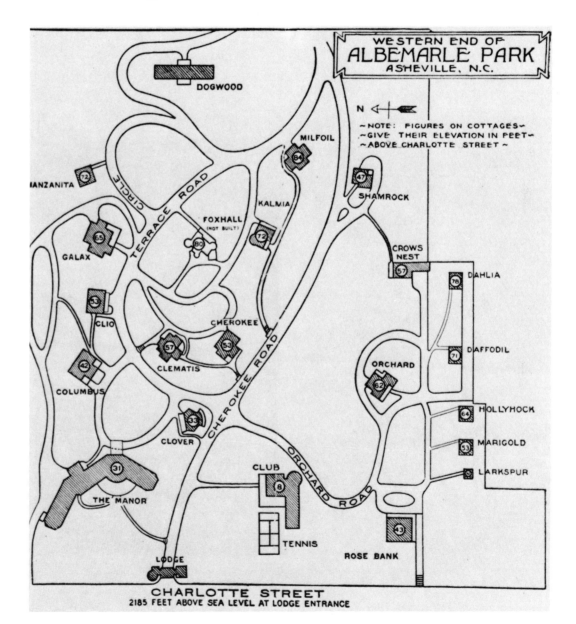

WESTERN END OF
ALBEMARLE PARK
ASHEVILLE, N.C.

~NOTE: FIGURES ON COTTAGES~
~GIVE THEIR ELEVATION IN FEET~
~ABOVE CHARLOTTE STREET~

CHARLOTTE STREET
2185 FEET ABOVE SEA LEVEL AT LODGE ENTRANCE

The Raoul children in later years, on the porch at Milfoil cottage. From left, Norman, Rebecca, Gaston, Mary, Loring, William Greene, Jr., Eleonore and Thomas.

Thomas had begun to take an active role in civic improvement projects in Asheville soon after The Manor opened. In 1900, he hired on as a foreman for Howland's road building company and was in charge of the improvements and paving of Charlotte Street and Chestnut Street. In early spring, 1901, he supervised the regrading of Charlotte Street and the re-laying of the streetcar line.

By mid-1901, he had become chairman of the Good Roads Commission, and was going to international expositions around the country on behalf of the city to learn about the newest macadamizing techniques.

He also took a strong role in the Board of Trade and, by early 1902, was the vice-president of the company which built the first City Auditorium (where the Thomas Wolfe Auditorium sits today).

In 1920, "just as the sale of Albemarle Park was being consummated, those in charge of the Vanderbilt Estate decided to promote a development to obtain profit from some of its idle acres. The Biltmore Estate Company was formed with Tom at its head. The central feature of this development was its very charming Country Club, surrounded by an eighteen hole golf course. Edging the course and facing the Club are many homes, one of which belongs to Tom, who, at this writing (1945) is still head of the Company." (Mary Raoul Millis, The Family of Raoul)

This became Biltmore Forest, the Asheville area's premier enclave for the wealthy.

According to his obituary, printed in The

Asheville Times on April 7, 1953, "Raoul, with Chauncey Beadle, walked over nearly every route that later was laid off into streets of Biltmore Forest. The pair planned most of the streets during their walks through what was then only a forest."

In later years he found satisfaction in his twenty years of service as Clerk of the Town of Biltmore Forest.

The Governor appointed him to the North Carolina Park Commission in 1933, which was charged with acquiring land for inclusion in the Great Smoky Mountains National Park. He served for 14 years.

Three years later he was appointed to the North Carolina Liquor Control Commission to study methods for the control and sale of alcoholic beverages in the state.

He had married Helen Doyle Bennett in 1910 and they had two daughters, Kathleen and Jane.

After a long illness, he died at the age of 76 on April 7, 1953.

The progressive civic-mindedness instilled in Thomas Wadley Raoul by his parents was, in turn, conveyed to his own daughters. Today, Jane Raoul Bingham, still residing in "Raoulwood," the Biltmore Forest home her father built in 1922, is active in a broad spectrum of community issues, ranging from the preservation of western North Carolina's scenic beauty to the care of people afflicted with Alzheimer's Disease and Parkinson's Disease.

"Raoulwood," the house Thomas Wadley Built for his family in Biltmore Forest. His wife, Helen, so loved the living room in Milfoil cottage, where they lived prior to leaving Albemarle Park, that he reproduced it here.

The Manor

The opening of the Grove Park Inn in 1913 presaged the slow decline that was to befall The Manor during the late 1920s and early 1930s.

The Manor continued hosting the regular guests who had been coming for years to spend entire seasons in Asheville, but it attracted fewer and fewer new visitors as the Grove Park Inn flourished.

Christmas Day, 1935, was the last good day, with fifty guests staying at The Manor, according to Albert Malone, son of the Raouls' last manager of The Manor, A.H. Malone. After 1936, coal became so expensive, according to him, and the ever rising cost of heating the place made it and more difficult to keep the operation profitable.

The Manor changed hands numerous times from the mid-1930s on.

By 1940, it had closed.

On March 25, 1920, a small attic fire broke out at The Manor, creating quite a spectacle for observers on Edwin Place. Repair of the damage began less than 24 hours after the fire was extinguished.

It reopened in 1944, having undergone a major upfitting by new investors. In the late 1940s it enjoyed a renewed vitality, with prominent guests that included Grace Kelly, Alec Guinness, Agnes Morehead and Louis Jordan who were in Asheville to film <u>The Swan</u> on the grounds of the Biltmore Estate.

In 1961, Charles Lavin converted it to a retirement hotel, one of forty registered retirement hotels in the country. The swimming pools that had been added in the mid-1950s became the center of a separately managed pool and bath club that was very popular in the community.

By 1976, the Manor had changed hands again, this time to become a general residential hotel. The ballroom was used for judo classes and, later, dance performances. The Pump Room, a restaurant during the 1950s, was used for local theatrical shows. The large dining room became home for the Stone Soup Restaurant.

In 1984, after two brutal winters had wreaked havoc on the steam pipes, water lines and sprinkler system, the Manor was finally closed.

The Preservation Society of Asheville and Buncombe County bought The Manor along with Clover and Columbus cottages and the greensward along Cherokee Road that had become a parking lot for the Inn in 1989, when the owner had threatened demolition of the structures. The Society aggressively marketed the property nationwide for more than two years, showing it to more than a hundred prospective buyers.

In May, 1991, it succeeded in attracting a buyer who, at the time this book was going to press (August, 1991), was converting it into 52 apartments.

In July, 1991, the Manor was used as one of the locations for the filming <u>The Last of the Mohicans</u>, featuring the actor Daniel Day Lewis. Hundreds of local residents were extras and, for a few days, The Manor and a part of Albemarle Park became mid-18th century Albany, New York, with British red-

A relaxed afternoon outdoors under the linden tree on The Manor's tiled east patio.

coats, "indians," and dozens of colonials filling the streets.

The Cottages

From the very start, the Raouls offered to sell building lots in Albemarle Park and build cottages for investors.

In 1913, they replatted the property and, within a year, sold off the lots on which Fox Hall, Breezemont, Wildfell and several other cottages were built.

The Manor Inn in the 1970s, operated as a retirement hotel, with a separate Pool and Bath Club open to the neighborhood.

In 1920, when E.W. Grove bought the property it only included eleven of the cottages and about half of the thirty-six acres.

Each time The Manor sold, fewer cottages accompanied it. By 1944, the property included only five cottages and twelve acres.

Today, Clover and Columbus cottages and about four acres are still part of The Manor property.

By 1917, there were thirty-five structures in Albemarle Park—the Inn, the Clubhouse and numerous cottages.

Five more cottages were built by 1925, four more by 1945 and only five more by the early 1960s.

While many of the cottages have been remodeled, only one has been substantially altered from its original appearance—Larkspur

cottage. Most of the other changes have been in character with the predominant design style of the cottage at the time of its construction.

Of all the buildings that were built in Albemarle Park from its inception in 1897, only the following are gone: Locust Cottage's garage, Fir Tree's garage, a servant's building along the service drive north of The Manor, the stable behind Clio and Galax, the

In 1991, The Manor was briefly transformed into Albany, New York in the 1750s, for location filming of <u>The Last of the Mohicans</u>.

Public Garage near Charlotte Street, a garage near Breezemont, and most recently, The Manor Boiler House, which was removed to provide vehicular access from Charlotte Street for the apartments being developed in The Manor Inn.

The Clubhouse

In the late 1950s, Logan Robertson converted the Clubhouse, with its billiards room and bowling alley, into the Medical Arts Building, enclosing sections of the original building to provide more interior space. The tennis court became a parking lot.

Today, it's a professional office park. Three "rondettes" were added to the property in the 1950s, perched on the bank near the parking lot, to provide additional office space.

The Landscape

As the cottages became permanent residences, and their owners sought more privacy, several of the secondary roads and interconnecting paths were abandoned, given over to lawn or woods.

The roadways that emerged from the service drive behind The Manor and ascended the mountainside behind Galax and Manzanita no longer exist, and the paths and alleys that served the Border Row Cottages have long since been altered. The drive behind Orchard Cottage and the small entry drives to Rosebank and Shamrock have also been altered and absorbed into the private realm of each cottage's site.

However, the original character of the landscape remains unchanged. Even as the newer cottages of the 1940s and 1950s were built, attention was paid to proper siting, to preserve the original intent of the Park.

Many of the significant trees are in their maturity and some of the understory plantings have disappeared or been overwhelmed by newer, more invasive species.

Postscript

In a few years, Albemarle Park will celebrate its centennial. Enormous change can occur in one hundred years. A community can develop and disintegrate in as little time as that, and disappear from the map without leaving behind a trace of its existence. That's the nature of boom towns. Coal camps in Kentucky, gold mining towns in Colorado, logging communities in Washington, many of them are gone. The boom died and people moved on.

Asheville was a boom town, too, when Albemarle Park was developed and The Manor and Cottages were built. Luckily, Albemarle Park has not suffered that fate. Every one of its significant structures remains, relatively unchanged from when they were built. The landscape, though in a mature phase now, is also relatively intact.

All of Albemarle Park is a historic district listed in the National Register of Historic Places (1977) and all but four properties are part of The Albemarle Park Local Historic District (1989). The Manor and Gatehouse are also individually designated Local Historic Properties. With these protections in place the design integrity of this community will endure.

Residents and visitors alike can continue to enjoy, for many years, the special quality one finds in Albemarle Park, a quality that four imaginative men were able to create out of a small tenant farm in the mountains of North Carolina in the late 1890s.

Albemarle Park in its hey-day, ca. 1921. The Lodge at Charlotte Street with The Manor Inn behind, when the street was still paved with brick and the streetcars were running.

Planned Communities: Placing Albemarle Park in Context

Albemarle Park is a significant historic landscape in the evolution of residential community design in the United States. To determine its full significance, it's best to examine it within the context of the American planning movement, as part of a brief chronology of renowned American planned communities.

The development of the English suburb had begun fifty to a hundred years earlier than its American counterparts. However, when designers here began to develop their own versions of the planned community, their approach was more "picturesque" in character.

In 1869, Frederick Law Olmsted and Calvert Vaux, most widely known for their design of Central Park in New York City, developed a scheme for a "suburban village" in Illinois titled the General Plan for Riverside. It promoted the principles of curvilinear road design over the conventional rectangular grid and the use of underground drainage systems. Both of these developments influenced the design of future communities such as Albemarle Park.

During this time, several books were published that reinforced the growing realization that there was aesthetic and economic value to be found in preserving the natural terrain and landscape.

As designers and developers jointly embraced these concepts, the construction of

The first letterhead of The Albemarle Park Company, showing the Lodge as viewed from Cherokee Road.

American planned communities burgeoned. The design of Albemarle Park was, no doubt, influenced by those communities that preceded it; however, it also contributes to our planning knowledge. It demonstrates how problems that are unique to residential development on rugged mountainous terrain can be solved.

The following list is a portion of the legacy of influential residential planned communities in the United States. The design of today's modern subdivisions has evolved from these early, landmark communities. Unfortunately, the sound planning principles developed in these historic models have often been lost or overlooked by modern developers. It's hoped that, by looking at models like Albemarle Park, we can begin to improve the design of the communities in which we live.

Listed chronologically, these first American planned communities, in most cases, were comprehensively designed by teams of allied professionals that included planners, landscape architects, architects and engineers.

Albemarle Park benefitted from such a team in the landscape architect Samuel Parsons, Jr., architect Bradford Gilbert, engineer George E. Waring, and the developer William Greene Raoul. Although, today, its place in the distinguished chronology below may come as a surprise, it would be solely due to its lack of national exposure. The historic record portrayed in this publication and Albemarle Park's greatly extant residential community should earn it a place in our heritage alongside these better known masterworks.

1853 LLEWELLYN PARK,
West Orange, New Jersey
Andrew Jackson Davis, Architect

1856 LAKE FOREST, Illinois
Jed Hotchkiss, Landscape Architect

1869 RIVERSIDE, Illinois
Frederick Law Olmsted, Calvert Vaux,
Olmsted, Vaux & Co., NY

1869 GARDEN CITY, New York

1872 PARKSIDE, Buffalo, New York
F.L. Olmsted and George Radford
(partially constructed)

1880 PULLMAN, Illinois
Nathan F. Barrett, Landscape Architect,
Solon Spencer Beman, Architect

1880 SHORT HILLS, New Jersey

1885 ROCHELLE PARK,
New Rochelle, New York
Nathan F.Barrett, Landscape Architect

1885, TUXEDO PARK,
Tuxedo Park, New York
Bruce Price, Architect

1891 ROLAND PARK, Baltimore, Maryland
George E. Kessler and Olmsted and Olmsted,
Landscape Architects
(additional section by Charles Platt)

1897 ALBEMARLE PARK,
Asheville, North Carolina
Samuel Parsons Jr., Landscape Architect,
Bradford Gilbert, Architect

1899 PROSPECT PARK SOUTH,
Brooklyn, New York
John Aitkin, Landscape Architect,
John J. Petit, Architect

1906 BEVERLY HILLS, California
Wilbur D. Cook, Landscape Architect

1912 FOREST HILLS GARDENS,
Queens, New York
Olmsted Brothers, Landscape Architects
and Grosvenor Atterbury, Architect

1913 COUNTRY CLUB DISTRICT,
Kansas City, Missouri
Hare and Hare, Landscape Architects

1916 MOSS HILL, Boston, Massachusetts
Pray, Hubbard and White,
Landscape Architects

1918 BRIDGEPORT HOUSING,
Bridgeport, Connecticut
Arthur A. Shurtleff, Planner,
R. Clipston Sturgis, Architect

1918 MARIEMONT NEW TOWN,
Cincinnati, Ohio
John Nolen, Town Planner,
Philip Foster, Associate

1918 UNION PARK GARDENS,
Wilmington, Delaware
John Nolen

1922 ROCKWOOD, Cincinnati, Ohio
Albert Davis Taylor, Landscape Architect
and Town Planner

1924 SUNNYSIDE GARDENS,
Queens, New York
Clarence Stein and Henry Wright, Planners,
Frederick L. Ackerman

1925 VENICE BEACH, Venice, Florida
John Nolen

1928 RADBURN, Radburn, New Jersey
Clarence Stein and Henry Wright,
planners/architects, Marjorie Cautley,
Landscape Architect

1935 GREENBELT, Maryland
Hale Walker, Planner, Douglas D. Ellington
and R.J. Wedsworth, Architects

1941 BALDWIN HILLS VILLAGE,
Los Angeles, California
Clarence Stein, Planner, Reginald D. Johnson
and Wilson, Merrill and Alexander,
Architects

This chronology was developed with assistance from Charles A. Birnbaum, ASLA.

A Chronology of Structures in Albemarle Park

Though there exists quite a bit of information available to us today, it's still not possible to accurately date the construction or loss of every structure in Albemarle Park. The chronological list below was developed from the following sources:

The Letters of Thomas Wadley Raoul
The Raoul Family Papers
The Maps of the Sanborn Insurance Company, Ltd. (Feb., 1901; June, 1907; July, 1913; Nov., 1917; Feb., 1925; 1945.)
The Buncombe County Record of Deeds
The Asheville City Directories
Conversations with Lucile Barkley

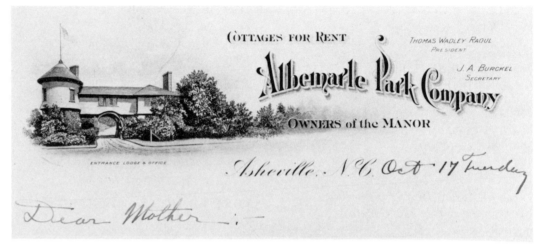

A later version of Albemarle Park letterhead. This time, the Charlotte Street facade of the Lodge was used.

The Lodge	1898
Columbus	1898
Clover	1898
The Manor Inn	1898
Milfoil	1898
Shamrock	1898
Orchard	1899
Clio	1900
Clematis (Laurel)	1901
1st servants' bldg.	1901
Galax	1902
The Clubhouse	1902
First addition to The Manor	1903
(The Charlotte Street wing)	
Cherokee	1903
Rosebank	1905
Crow's Nest	1905
Dahlia	1906
Daffodil	1906
Larkspur (moved to current site)	1906
Manzanita	1906
Hollyhock	1907
Marigold	1907
2nd servants' building	1907
Stable	1909
Dogwood	1910
Kalmia	1910
Fox Hall and Fox Den	1913
Second addition to The Manor Inn	1913

(The Terrace Road wing)	
Breezemont	1913
Alva Glen	1913
Possum Trot	1913
Brown Bear (originally Wren's Nest)	1914
Wildfell	1914
Raven's Nest	1916
Fir Tree	1917
Locust	1917
Snug Harbor	1917
Pine Tree	1917
Addition to 1st servants' bldg.	1917
Addition to stable	1917
The Manor boiler house	1917
Public garage	1917
Breezemont 2nd garage	1918
Possum Trot garage	1920
Chipmunk	1922
Chestnut Hill	1922
Twin Oaks	1922
The Willows	1925
Fir Tree garage	1925
Snug Harbor Garage 1925	
Addition to Manor public garage	1925
Kalmia garage	1925
Manzanita garage	1938

Chipmunk garage	1940
Alva Glen garage	1945
Fruit Tree	1946
Italdo	1946
Seven Oaks	1947
Galax garage	1950
Cardinal	1951
Wakerobin	1954
Beech Tree	1964
Chestnut Hill garage	1963
Orchard garage	?
Three rondettes	1955

Losses

Part of stable	1925
Stable (stone foundation remains)	1940
1st servants' building	1945
The Manor public garage	1945
(The addition remains)	
Breezemont 2nd garage	1969
(foundation remains)	
Locust Garage	?
Fir Tree Garage	?
Orchard garage	1990
The Manor boiler house	1991

Albemarle Park
Planting List

From Samuel Parsons'
How To Plan The Home Grounds

Compiled by Al Kopf, ASLA and Clay Mooney, ASLA

Trees:

Green Ash - Fraxinus pennsylvanica
White Ash - Fraxinus americana
Tulip Tree - Liriodendron tulipifera
American Linden - Tilia americana
Pin Oak - Quercus palustris
Chestnut Oak - Quercus prinus
Black Cherry - Prunus serotina
Red Maple - Acer rubrum
Sugar Maple - Acer saccharum
Silver Maple - Acer saccharinum
Boxelder - Acer negundo
Oriental Plane Tree - Platanus orientalis

Shrubs:

Winter Honeysuckle - Lonicera fragrantissima
Common or Eastern Ninebark - Spiraea opulifolia =
    Physocarpus opulifolius
Forsythia - Forsythia suspensa var. fortunei
Virginia Sweetspire - Itea virginica
Indian Currant or Coralberry - Symphoricarpos glomerata
    or Symphoricarpos orbiculatus
Sweet Mock orange - Philadelphus coronarius
Red Osier Dogwood or Red twigged Dogwood - Cornus
    sericea or Cornus stolonifera Chinese Privet -
    Ligustrum sinense
Thorny Elaeagnus - Elaegnus pungens
Cherry Elaeagnus - Elaegnus multiflora
Japanese Barberry - Berberis thunbergii
Flame Azalea - Rhododendron calendulaceum
Pinkshell Azalea - Rhododendrom vaseyi
Swamp Azalea - Rhododendron viscosum

Vines:

Wisteria - Wisteria frutescens
English Ivy - Hedera helix
Prairie Rose - Rosa setigera
Virginia Creeper - Parthenocissus quinquefolia
Running Rose - Rosa

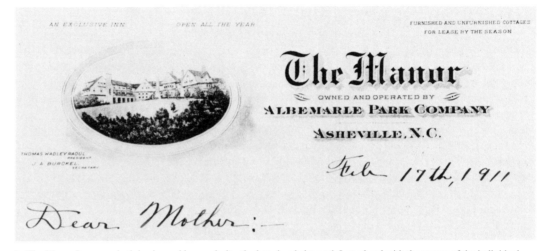

As The Manor Inn grew, both in size and in popularity, the letterhead changed. Letterhead with the names of the individual cottages was also available to the guests.

**Other Plants Mentioned in Raoul Family
    Correspondence:**

Wichuriana Rose (Memorial Rose) - Rosa wichuraiana
Norway Spruce - Picea abies
Scarlet Firethorn - Crateaegus pryacantha = Pyracantha
    coccinea
Sunflowers - Helianthus
Thorne
Iris
Tulips
Joncquils
Rhododendrons
Lilacs
Nasturtiums
Camperdown Elm - Ulmus x vegeta "camperdownii"

Evergreen Shrubs recommended by Parsons:

American Holly - Ilex opaca
Japanese Holly - Ilex crenata
Leatherleaf Mahonia - Mahonia bealei
Oregon Grapeholly - Berberis aquifolia = Mahonia
    aquifolium
Chinese Mahonia - Mahonia fortunei

Rhododendron "Mrs. C.S. Sargent" - R. catawbiense
    cultivar
Rhododendron x Everestianum - (from R. catawbiense)
Mountain Laurel - Kalmia latifolia
Andromedas (Mountain Pieris) - Pieris floribunda =
    Andromedas catesbii

Sources:

Hortus Third - Cornell University
Manual of Woody Landscape Plants - Michael Dirr

References/Bibliography

John Preston Arthur, <u>Western North Carolina: A History from 1730 to 1913</u> (Raleigh, NC: Edwards & Broughton Printing Co. 1914)

T. M. Barker, Jr.,<u>The Nutshell Guide to Asheville</u> (Feb., 1899)

Ora Blackmun, <u>Western North Carolina: Its Mountains and Its People to 1880</u> (Boone, N.C.: Appalachian Consortium Press, 1977)

J. M. Campbell, <u>Asheville - Nature's Sanitarium</u> (Asheville, N.C.: Real Estate Dealer's Promotional Brochure, 1899)

George H. Chapin, <u>Health Resorts of the South</u> (Boston, 1891)

William Phillips Comstock and Clarence Eaton Schermerhorn, <u>Bungalows, Camps and Mountain Houses</u> (Washington, D.C.: The American Institute of Architects
      Press [1908/1915] 1990 Reprint with an introduction by Tony P. Wrenn) Pg. VIII, XII.

Bradford L. Gilbert, <u>Architectural Sketches</u> (New York: Self-published, 1889)

Clay Lancaster, <u>The American Bungalow, 1880-1930</u> (New York: Abbeville Press 1985) Pg. 67, 239, 242.

Arnold Lewis, <u>American Country Houses of the Gilded Age (Sheldon's "Artistic Country Seats")</u> (New York: Dover Publications, Inc. [1886-87] 1982 Reprint.)

Mary Raoul Millis, <u>The Family of Raoul</u> (Privately Printed 1943)

Samuel Parsons, Jr., <u>How to Plan the Home Grounds</u> (New York: Doubleday & McClure Co., 1899)

Samuel Parsons, Jr., <u>Landscape Gardening Studies</u>, (New York: John Lane Company, 1910)

Samuel Parsons, Jr., <u>Landscape Gardening</u>, (New York, London: G.P. Putnam's Sons, 1891)

Samuel Parsons, <u>The Art of Landscape Architecture In Development and its Application to Modern Landscape Gardening</u>, (New York and London: G.P. Putnam's
      Sons, The Knickerbocker Press, 1915)

The Raoul Family Letters (Special Collections Division, Robert W. Woodruff Library, Emory University, Atlanta, Georgia)

Thomas Wadley Raoul's Letters (Jane Raoul Bingham's private collection)

Vincent J. Scully, Jr., <u>The Shingle Style and The Stick Style Revised Edition</u> (New Haven and London: Yale University Press [1955] 1971) Pg. 73.

F. A. Sondley, <u>A History of Buncombe County, North Carolina</u> (Asheville, N.C. : The Reprint Co.,[1930] 1977)

Gustav Stickley, Editor, <u>Craftsman Bungalows - 59 Homes from "The Craftsman"</u> (New York: Dover Publications, Inc. [Dec. 1903 - Aug. 1916] 1988 Reprint.) Pg.
      1, 4.

Doug Swaim, Editor, <u>Cabins & Castles The History & Architecture of Buncombe County, North Carolina</u> (Asheville, N.C.: The Historic Resources Commission of
      Asheville & Buncombe County, 1981)

<u>Asheville - Land of the Sky</u> (Asheville, N.C.: The Asheville Board of Trade, 1898)

<u>A History of Real Estate, Building and Architecture in New York City</u> (New York: Arno [1898] 1967 Reprint.)

<u>The National Cyclopedia of American Biography</u>, Vol. XIV Pg. 298-9; Vol. XXVI Pg. 308.(New York: James T. White Co.)

<u>American Architect & Building News</u>, Volume 14;

<u>Asheville City Directories</u>

<u>The Asheville Citizen</u>

<u>The Asheville Times</u>

<u>Building</u>, Volume 8, Number 1; Volume 8, Number 3;

Sanborn Insurance Maps Feb., 1901, June, 1907, 1913, Nov., 1917, 1925, 1945.(Sanborn Map Company, Ltd.)

Buncombe County Record of Deeds, Buncombe County Court House

Photograph/Illustration Credits

North Carolina Collection, Pack Memorial Library, Asheville, North Carolina, Pages 6, 7, 9, 20, 25, 27, 30, 32, 33(except top left), 34, 38, 46, 47, 48, 54, 64, 79 (?), 86, 91 (bottom), 100 (left), 101, 109.

E.H. Ball Photo Collection of the Southern Highlands Research Center at UNCA (University of North Carolina at Asheville), Asheville, North Carolina, Page 37, 39, 103.

Raoul Family Papers, The Special Collections Division, Robert W. Woodruff Library, Emory University, Atlanta, Georgia, Pages 5, 12, 13, 14, 15, 16, 17,1 9, 22 (right), 23, 24, 26, 29, 40, 44, 49, 58, 63, 70, 71, 74, 80, 87, 93, 94, 96, 98, 99.

Lavin Collection, North Carolina Department of Cultural Resources, Division of Archives and History, Raleigh, North Carolina, Pages 66, 67, 68, 78, 88.

The National Cyclopedia of American Biography, Pages 18, 41.

The Ernest Stevenson Bird Library, Fine Arts and Architecture Office, Syracuse University, Syracuse, New York, Page 21, 22 (left).

Buncombe County Record of Deeds, Buncombe County Courthouse, Page 43.

Jane Raoul Bingham, Pages 36, 42, 55 (?), 61, 89, 90, 92, 95, 104, 106, 107.

Charles Birnbaum, ASLA, Pages 45, 57, 59.

Fred Kahn, Pages 31, 72, 77 (left), 83 (left), 97, 110.

Charles and Cherry Livengood, Page 82.

Albert Malone, Pages 50, 100 (right).

Jane and Rich Mathews, Pages 2, 3, 8, 10, 11, 28, 33(top left), 35, 51, 52, 53, 56, 60, 62, 65, 69, 73, 75, 76, 77 (right), 83 (right), 84, 85, 91 (top), 102.

From the earliest days of Albemarle Park's development, Thomas Wadley Raoul was advertising its features in the Asheville City Directories.

The cover of a small promotional brochure advertising The Manor and cottages.

Acknowledgements

In June of 1988, the Albemarle Park - Manor Grounds Association was organized to protect and enhance the special landscape and architectural character of the Albemarle Park community. Concerned about the future of The Manor Inn, the centerpiece of Albemarle Park, which had been vacant for almost four years, the neighborhood petitioned the City of Asheville in January of 1989 to designate Albemarle Park a local historic district. This would afford the neighborhood greater protection through the adoption of architectural and landscape design guidelines and the regulation of modifications to the structures and grounds of Albemarle Park.

The neighborhood began, then, to gather all existing historical data it could find to enlarge upon the history of Albemarle Park, which was designated a National Register Historic District in 1977. It was through this research by the Association that information was uncovered revealing the important design collaboration of Samuel Parsons, an original founder of the American Society of Landscape Architects (ASLA), with architect Bradford Gilbert in the development of this "residential park" design at the turn of the century.

In December, 1989, the Asheville City Council designated Albemarle Park a local historic district, electing to omit four significant properties from the district - Locust, Fir Tree and Rosebank cottages, and the original Clubhouse for the Manor.

With this document, the Albemarle Park - Manor Grounds Association hopes to foster an appreciation and understanding of quality design by providing all readers with a case study of the foundations of planned residential communities. In a day and time when the modern residential development is so often a series of duplicate homes on grids of similar streets, Albemarle Park offers a refreshing look at the original design concepts for planned communities. Albemarle Park can be an example to other communities, as well as to developers, architects, planners and landscape professionals, and can be a guide to how land and building resources, especially in the mountains, can be used to enhance and improve the livability of residential communities.

This architectural and landscape history of Albemarle Park will serve as the critical basis for the historic district design guidelines created to guide ongoing and future rehabilitation and infill construction, protecting the integrity of the original design.

This book has been an almost two year project of the Albemarle Park-Manor Grounds Association. It is an effort that could not have been accomplished without the generous help of many members of the Asheville community and other friends of the neighborhood around the state and the country.

Acknowledgements (cont.)

Jane Raoul Bingham
Thomas Bingham
Albert Malone
Mrs. William Wood
Joseph and Justine Lavin, former owners of The Manor
R.L. Bailey, former owner of The Manor

The Members of the Albemarle Park/Manor Grounds Association and other residents of Albemarle Park
Lucile Barkley, Chipmunk Cottage
Mark, Debra and Zachry Bennett, Fox Hall Cottage
Vann and Kathy Gibbs, Pine Tree Cottage
Bruce and Eric Johnson and Lydia Jeffries, Breezemont Cottage
Charles and Cherry Livengood, Orchard Cottage
Rob Pulleyn, Galax Cottage
William and Sandra Simpson, Crow's Nest Cottage
Don and Joan Tracy, Dogwood Cottage

The Historic Resources Commission of Asheville & Buncombe County, Kent Newell, Executive Director
The City of Asheville Department of Parks and Recreation, Al Kopf, ASLA, Landscape Planner
The City of Asheville Planning Department

Mala Rao, planner, and Scott Fowler and Mary Weber, planning technicians
Pack Memorial Library, North Carolina Collection, Asheville, North Carolina
Lewis Buck, Laura Gaskin, Anna Donnally, librarians
The Preservation Society of Asheville & Buncombe County
The American Institute of Architects, Asheville Section of the North Carolina Chapter
The American Society of Landscape Architects, Committee on Historic Preservation
Patricia O'Donnell, ASLA and Noel Dorsey Vernon, ASLA
The North Carolina Department of Cultural Resources, Division of Archives & History, Western Regional Office, Martha Fullington
The Special Collections Division, Robert W. Woodruff Library, Emory University, Atlanta, Georgia
The Ernest Stevenson Bird Library, Fine Arts and Architecture Office, Syracuse University, Syracuse, New York Barbara Opar, librarian and Andrea Kosmo, assistant
Avery Architecture and Fine Arts Library, Columbia University, New York City, New York

The Community Foundation of Western North Carolina, Inc.
The Marion Stedman Covington Foundation
The National Trust for Historic Preservation
The North Carolina Arts Council, Design Arts Program, Deborah Eagle, Design Arts Coordinator,

Peter Alberice, AIA
John Broadbooks, ASLA
Fred Kahn
Cleve and Marion Mathews
Clay Mooney, ASLA
Dr. Lowell Orbison
John Reid
Altamont Press, Asheville, North Carolina, Rob Pulleyn and Elaine Thompson
The Education Center, Greensboro, North Carolina, Dr. Albert J. and Marge Michel
Henco Drafting and Art Supplies, Inc., Jim Carson
Quality Forward, Susan Roderick
SPACEPLAN/Architecture, Interiors & Planning, P.A., Asheville, North Carolina
VMS Business Systems, Asheville, North Carolina, Mark Bennett

Index